For Judyth, and John

IMPORTANT BILLING AND CREDIT REQUIREMENTS

All producers of the play *must* give credit to the author of the play in all programs distributed in connection with performances of the play and in all instances in which the title of the play appears for purposes of advertising, publicizing or otherwise exploiting the play and/or a production. The name of the author *must* also appear on a separate line, on which no other name appears, immediately following the title, and *must* appear in size of type not less than fifty percent the size of the title type. Biographical information on the author, if included in the playbook, may be used in all programs. *In all programs this notice must appear:*

Produced by special arrangement with
THE DRAMATIC PUBLISHING COMPANY of Woodstock, Illinois

The development of VOICES FROM THE SHORE was supported by the Children's Theater Foundation of America with an Aurand Harris Playwriting grant.

VOICES FROM THE SHORE WAS selected as a 2003 finalist in the Plays in Our Schools program sponsored by the American Alliance of Theater and Education and received a workshop in March of 2003 at Grandview High School, in Denver, Colorado. Grandview subsequently fully produced the play in February 2004, under the direction of Dr. Michael Pearl.

VOICES FROM THE SHORE was co-commissioned by Penn Charter High School in Philadelphia, Pennsylvania, and Lawrence High School in Lawrence, Kansas. On November 17, 2000, it opened at Penn Charter with the following cast and crew:

Joel	Karl Blumenthal
Lucas	John Sullivan-Rivera
Beth	Colette Oldham
Laura	Carly Keidel
Trisha	Catherine Pappas
Holly	Jennie Rosen
Rick	Chris Covollo
Julie	Abby Mann
Tom	Michael Candelori
Coby	Julia Soffa
Katherine	Lauren Edgerton
Ghost	David Erlbaum
Demon	Matt Volk
Dying Girl	Hillary Bennet

Director . . . . Eva Kay Noone
Assistant to Director . . . . Chrisina Rose
Set Designer . . . . Dirk Durosette
Stage Crew Advisor . . . . Michael Roche
Costume Designer . . . . Millie Hubel
Lighting Designer . . . . Krista Billings
Percussion Composition & Performance . . Jeremy Schilling
Stage Manager . . . . Ryan Liddell
Production Manager . . . . Jessi Stein
Light Board Operator . . . . Hannah Baumgartner
Sound Board Operator . . . . Ben Gillespie
Poster and Program Cover Design . . . . Matt Volk
Ticket Design . . . . Jerome Wright
Running Crew . . . . Devra Friedman, Melissa Lucas

VOICES FROM THE SHORE opened at Lawrence High
School on October 25, 2001, with the following cast and
crew:

Joel . . . . Peter Clark
Lucas . . . . Ely Fair
Beth . . . . Julie Thomas
Laura . . . . Brianna Orton
Trisha . . . . Caitlin Welch
Holly . . . . Kasey Ross
Rick . . . . Jason Russell
Julie . . . . Tyler Levy
Tom . . . . Wesley Teal
Coby . . . . Ashley Crowder
Katherine . . . . Jeni Phillips
Ghost . . . . Kenith Easthouse
Demon . . . . Dennis Mersmann

6

Dying Girl . . . . Asha Park-Carter

Director . . . . Jeanne Averill
Technical Director & Lighting Design . . . Heather Schmidt
Assistant Directors . . . . . . Ariel Clark, Michael Monaghan
Stage Managers . . . . Kayla Bennett, Ashley Jones
Set . . . . Kayla Bennett, Ashley Jones, Erica Fisher,
          Erin Niedenthal, Kasey Ross, Tyler Levy, Wesley Teal
Props . . . . . Jeni Phillips, Heidi Haynes, Dennis Mersmann
Sound . . Michael Bradford, Kenith Easthouse, Sara Miller,
                          Asha Park-Carter, Kellyn Young
Publicity . . Ashley Crowder, Will Brubaker, Jason Russell,
                          Julie Thomas, Caitlin Welch
Lights . . . . Brianna Orton, Justin Bullock, Peter Clark,
                          Rachel Hillmer
Costumes . . . . Ely Fair

SONG CREDITS (music in back of book): Original music and
lyrics by Dale Dieleman.

ACKNOWLEDGMENTS

I thank the following for their invaluable help in the creation of
Voices From the Shore: Judyth Miller, Melissa Warner, Amber
Bosier, Robert Para, Eva Kay Noone, Steve Townsend, Jeanne
Averill, David Vanderschuur, Rosanne Steffens, Dawn High-
house, Amy Volkers, Deborah Schakel, Robin Nott, T.J.
Rathburn, Margaret Russell, Ross Heflin, Krystal Roberts, Amy
Syversen, Ryan Hebert, Sarah Cupper, Lexi Rathburn, Emily
Hanavan, Kaneen Geiger, Brad DeLong, Alexis Hollin, Logan
Higley, Chrystal Smith, Michael Pearl, Patrick Foley, Patricia
Zimmer, Scott Mead, Ric Roberts, Rachel Briley, Richard King,
Dale Dieleman, Sandy Asher.

VOICES FROM THE SHORE

A Play in Two Acts
For 6 Men and 8 Women

CHARACTERS

LUCAS . . . . 17-18, Joel's best friend
JOEL . . . . 17-18, Lucas' best friend
BETH . . . . 17-18, Joel's girlfriend
LAURA 17-18
TRISHA 17-18
HOLLY 17-18
RICK . . . . 18, Holly's boyfriend
JULIE . . . . 17-18, resident of the psych ward
TOM . . . . 17-18, resident of the psych ward
COBY . . . . 17-18, resident of the psych ward
KATHERINE. . . . . 17-18, resident of the psych ward
VOICES:
    GHOST . . . . of 17-18-year-old male
    DEMON
    DYING GIRL 17-18

PLACE: Joel's beach and the day room in an acute-care, locked, adolescent psychiatric ward.

TIME: ACT I, SCENE I: Spring vacation, this school year. Dusk. SCENE II: A couple of hours later. ACT II, SCENE I: 3 days later. SCENE II: 4 weeks later.

Approximate running time: 1 hour, 35 minutes.

ACT I

SCENE I

SCENE: *The first Saturday of spring vacation in March. The beach just before sunset.*

AT RISE: *JOEL enters, followed by LUCAS. Already out on the beach are a picnic table with snacks on it and a larger cooler.*

LUCAS *(carrying as many lawn chairs and beach chairs as is humanly possible)*. Talk to me.

JOEL. I don't have to talk to you; you're my friend.

LUCAS. Friends talk to each other; that's why they're friends.

JOEL. Because you're my friend I don't have to talk to you.

LUCAS. All right, then I'll talk to myself. Why won't he talk to me about Beth? And why did I carry all the chairs and he didn't carry any? *(He drops all the chairs, answers himself.)* It's his beach. Oh, yeah.

JOEL. Beth wants me to talk to her, too. She wants me to tell her all my fears and doubts.

LUCAS. Ooo, dangerous. *(He sets up chairs around beach during following.)*

JOEL. If I did that to her—that would be like somebody throwing up in your shoes.

9

LUCAS. Joel, *(He laughs.)* I'm sorry I threw up in your shoes. You don't forget anything! We were seven years old!

JOEL. You could have told me before I put them on.

LUCAS. Joel, something happened with Beth and I got to know what it is or I can't help you.

JOEL. Beth and I were in her room while her parents were gone—

LUCAS *(suddenly very interested)*. What?

JOEL. —and we were listening to music—

LUCAS. Oh, yeah!

JOEL. and— Does this ever happen to you?

LUCAS. Not enough.

JOEL. I was kissing her and…

LUCAS. And?

JOEL. and I started to get a headache so I asked her to sing to me and she said no. So I left.

LUCAS. What? What-what-what? You left?

JOEL. Does that ever happen to you?

LUCAS. Sure, and then I throw up in their shoes and leave. You left?

JOEL. I know what you would have done.

LUCAS. What?

JOEL. The same thing you did to Juanita.

LUCAS. I would not smash her car!

JOEL. No, you'd write her a poem.

LUCAS *(proudly)*. Yeah.

JOEL. I wrote Beth a poem but it was stupid so I burned it.

LUCAS. That's what poetry is—stupid. All you got to do is say I luv you, and oh yeah, say something about her eyes. Like: *(Speaking to his bottle of soda.)*
    "I luv to see your beautiful eyes…

staring deep in my soul.
It makes me think of…
great rock and roll."

JOEL *(he laughs. LUCAS laughs)*. That is stupid. That's so damn stupid you'd probably send it.

LUCAS. Yeah. And it would work, too.

JOEL. That's what you wrote to Juanita?

LUCAS. Something like it.

JOEL. What did you use to rhyme with Lucas? No, don't tell me.

LUCAS. That's why I wrote it in Spanish. Using my Spanish name: El White Guy… *Bueno, no? Amor es mi vida.* *

JOEL. "She walks in beauty, like the night
        Of cloudless climes and starry skies;
        And all that's best of dark and bright
        Meet in her aspect and her eyes."

LUCAS. Not as good as mine, but you got it.

JOEL. I got it from Byron.

LUCAS. He won't care if you borrow it for a while. You want something to eat?

JOEL. No, I'm fasting.

LUCAS. Not eating?

JOEL. What does the word fasting mean?

LUCAS. Joel, first it was vitamins—

JOEL. I'm still taking them, you should try them, you might pass history.

LUCAS. Now you're fasting?

JOEL. I'm purifying my body.

LUCAS. Did the doctors say that would help?

JOEL. It will.

---

* Good, yes? Love is my life.

LUCAS. Is that what the clinic told you to do?

JOEL. Yeah.

LUCAS. How are you doing tonight?

JOEL. Better. I'm fasting. Is Laura coming tonight?

LUCAS *(in a sudden pain, at the sound of her name)*. Laura…

JOEL. Is she coming?

LUCAS. I wrote her notes, I called her, I sent her a hand-drawn invitation, I told her mother if she made Laura come I'd paint their house.

JOEL *(looking away, preoccupied with something internal)*. I thought she was going with Randy.

LUCAS. I think they're having problems.

JOEL *(distantly)*. Why?

LUCAS. When she looks at me, I feel my clothes disappearing.

JOEL. Why are you going after her, anyway?

LUCAS. She can talk.

JOEL. So can my grandmother.

LUCAS. Laura's fun to talk to because she's smart. Not just with grades, although she did better than me in Algebra.

JOEL. Everybody did better than you in Algebra.

LUCAS. I like the way she walks.

JOEL *(turning back to him)*. What part of her do you watch when she walks?

LUCAS *(grins)*. Her… *(His grin transforms into an expression of pain.)* Mind.

JOEL. Right. What if smart Laura asked you questions and she would know if you were lying?

LUCAS. That would scare me. Because if she knew everything about me she'd beat me with a stick.

JOEL. Why? What have *you* done?

LUCAS. Whatever it is, Laura wouldn't like it.

JOEL. Yeah, see? Beth knows.

LUCAS. Knows what?

JOEL. Women can read your mind, sometimes. *(Silence, as two worried young men contemplate this on the beach. They look away, then at each other and try to shake off their panic.)*

LUCAS. Do you remember in psychology class the day Anderson brought in those pictures and one of them looked like a young woman, but if you looked at it another way, it looked like an old woman? Then a young woman, the old woman, and the more you looked at it you couldn't figure out what it was.

JOEL. Yeah.

LUCAS. When I look at Laura, the same thing happens to me. Only instead of a young woman and an old woman, I see a young woman and some kind of space alien. *(Beat.)* I say "Hi, Laura" and she turns to me and says: *Uro pleb klatu barata*, and I fear for my life. A death ray's going to shoot out of her eyes and burn me into green gas.

JOEL. Yeah, so then you have to get up and leave.

LUCAS. No, it makes me want to kiss her.

JOEL. You're weird. You are very weird.

LUCAS. Maybe there's a course in college called Understanding Women.

JOEL. I'm not going to take it. I'd flunk. *(Beat.)* I want to take Understanding Myself.

LUCAS. I'd like you to take that course, too. *(Short silence.)*

JOEL. Did you sign up for summer orientation?

LUCAS *(moving away)*. Damn.

JOEL. What?

LUCAS. They turned me down, again.

JOEL. Who?

LUCAS. State.

JOEL. Oh, I know. I'm sorry.

LUCAS. How do you know?

JOEL. I could tell.

LUCAS. They said my dad makes too much at the Chrysler factory and my dad says he's got six kids, and can't afford it.

JOEL. I bet he feels terrible. He wants you to go—he wants you to pitch.

LUCAS. And they wouldn't increase my baseball scholarship. So, right after high school ends I'm going to have to w— *(He shivers.)*

JOEL. You're going to have to w—? *(He shivers.)*

LUCAS. I'll have to wo— *(He chokes.)*

JOEL. Wo—? *(He chokes.)*

LUCAS. wooorrrkkkrk full time. In the Chrysler factory.

JOEL. We have things to do this summer. It's our last summer before college. Who knows what's going to happen after we get there.

LUCAS. My mom says I should take the year off, earn some money— "You'll grow into yourself more. You'd be a better student." If I work in that factory for a year I'll grow into my dad. *(As his dad; suddenly adding weight.)* "Get me a beer! Where's my cigarettes? Turn on the TV, I gotta think!" I'll lose my scholarship if I wait a year. Even if I start in the winter. *(JOEL hasn't been listening and is lost in thought.)* Joel?

JOEL *(to himself)*. There are no fires.

LUCAS. What?

JOEL *(turning to LUCAS)*. Working all summer? You going to work at school, too?

LUCAS. I have to. Maybe I'll be a waitress. I'll get big tips.

JOEL. Your grades are bad enough; you just barely got into State. What are they going to be in college when you're working all the time?

LUCAS. Better, because I'll be more mature.

JOEL. What did you say? You'll be more manure?

LUCAS. Mature. Mature!

JOEL. I know, I was joking.

LUCAS. I know, I just couldn't believe you said that.

JOEL. It was funny.

LUCAS. Yeah, if you're my dad.

JOEL. I don't want to live in a dorm. There's too many people in a dorm. I want to live in an apartment.

LUCAS. I can't afford an apartment.

JOEL. I can't live in the dorm.

LUCAS. You're not thinking, Joel. We live in an apartment, who's going to cook? We'd have to order Chinese every night. I hate Chinese.

JOEL *(this is bad news and makes him anxious)*. Will you read to me?

LUCAS. I'm sorry, but I don't think I can stay—

JOEL. The sun is going down and you won't be able to see.

LUCAS. What do you want me to read?

JOEL. I brought *Rhyme of the Ancient Mariner*.

LUCAS. Haven't you got that memorized by now? Why don't you just recite one of your favorite parts. I'm sorry I don't have the money. If you need to live in an apartment, that's all right, but I can't afford it.

JOEL. I'll pay for it.

LUCAS. What?

JOEL. I'll pay for the whole apartment. You can't work while we're going to school. We've got too much to do.

LUCAS. You can't pay for my apartment. People don't do that.

JOEL. I got money.

LUCAS. You earned that money working in your father's office. You hate working in your father's office.

JOEL. And playing drums. I love playing drums.

LUCAS. You can't do that.

JOEL. College is going to be better than anything. I'll take every English and psychology class they have, you'll— what are you taking?

LUCAS. Understanding Women.

JOEL. You'll be doing whatever you want because it's just you and me in an apartment, and when we graduate, Beth will marry me, the university will hire me as a psychology professor, and you'll move next door and— what are you going to do after you graduate?

LUCAS. What's my degree going to be in?

JOEL. Social...izing.

LUCAS. So I'll move next door and you'll hire me to hang out with you.

JOEL. Yeah. So you can't be working all the time. *(Picking up gloves and baseball.)* You can't be a waitress. You have to be a pitcher. *(Throws glove to LUCAS.)*

LUCAS. That would break my heart, not working all the time.

JOEL *(as they get ready to play catch)*. Nothing is going to stop us from going to college.

LUCAS. All right.

JOEL. And once I move out, I'm never moving back here. They can drive each other crazy, instead of me. *(Throws ball to LUCAS. They play catch.)* Beth writes me notes.

LUCAS. Beth writes you notes.

JOEL. Yeah. *(Short silence.)*

LUCAS. Beth wrote you a note and said something that freaked you.

JOEL. I invited Trisha.

LUCAS. Where?

JOEL. Here.

LUCAS. Tonight? I thought you invited Beth.

JOEL. I invited Trisha and Beth.

LUCAS. Joel, what if they both come?

JOEL. I didn't think Beth would come and I didn't want to sit here and watch you with Laura, but then Beth wrote me a note and said she was coming— I invited Holly, too.

LUCAS. And Holly?

JOEL. Well, I hired her.

LUCAS *(stopping game)*. What did you ask her to do? What kind of party is this going to be?

JOEL *(throwing glove at LUCAS)*. I hired her to sing. I thought it would help me if I needed it.

LUCAS. Joel, you invited three women to the same party.

JOEL. I'm getting a headache.

LUCAS *(moving to him)*. No, no don't do that. It'll be all right. Beth and Laura will come, Trisha's car will break down, Holly will do whatever you hired her to do and we'll be grown men by morning.

JOEL *(in pain, holding his head)*. My forehead is swelling up. It is. Swelling; swelling way up.

LUCAS. Not tonight, Joel, not tonight.

JOEL. Why? Why do I get these?

LUCAS. What did the doctors say at that clinic?

JOEL. I think I have allergies; I have brain allergies.

LUCAS. Brain allergies? What are you allergic to?

JOEL *(still in pain)*. I don't know. I didn't fill out all my journals, I couldn't concentrate.

LUCAS. Joel, you read *War and Peace*. You can concentrate.

JOEL. And my mom, I shouldn't have brought her with me. She never stopped.

LUCAS. What did they find out?

JOEL *(still hurting, rubbing his forehead)*. Nothing.

LUCAS. Nothing? But you were there for a week. You had all those tests.

JOEL. Test after test after test and they can't find anything wrong. But I read the pamphlets, at the clinic, I read their books. My brain; it's allergic to something; maybe something I eat.

LUCAS. That's why you're fasting.

JOEL. What do you think?

LUCAS. I don't know, Joel. But if you start getting a headache or feeling weird or hearing stuff tonight, tell me right away, so I can help you. Where are your pills? *(Looking for them.)*

JOEL. They don't work.

LUCAS. Are they on the table? *(He finds them, holds them up.)* Do you want a couple now?

JOEL. Have you ever lied to me?

LUCAS. No. All right—wait… No.

JOEL. You didn't go out with Beth about four months ago when she was mad at me? Because you said you didn't.

JOEL *(putting pills down)*. Did I go out with Beth? Not really. All we did was talk about you.

JOEL. Did you tell me you were going to pay me back for that trip to Chicago, and you never did?

LUCAS. I can still do that; time's not up on that, yet; I'll still pay you.

JOEL. Did you put our cat in the dryer? And let my sister take the blame?

LUCAS. Yes. But I was not the one who turned it on!

JOEL. So, you'd tell me the truth if I asked you something important?

LUCAS. Yes. *(JOEL hesitates.)* Well?

JOEL. Did I ever…

(The pale and bloodied GHOST appears behind LUCAS. This stops JOEL, who stares at him. The GHOST is about JOEL's height, looks something like JOEL, is dressed very much like JOEL, and often will mirror JOEL's movements. Some of these movements are mentioned in the script. There is a large bloody wound in his chest near his heart.)

LUCAS. What?

GHOST. Tell him.

JOEL. I was…

GHOST. He's your friend.

LUCAS. What? What is it?

GHOST. Tell him what you did to me.

LUCAS. Joel, wake up, what do you want to ask me?

GHOST. And your headaches will go away.

JOEL *(to LUCAS)*. I have to know…

GHOST. There's blood on your hand. *(JOEL looks at his left hand, then at his right.)*

JOEL. Is there…do you see…?

LUCAS. Are you hearing something? Who are you listening to?

JOEL. I just thought there was blood on my hand.

LUCAS. Joel, you can't do this, tonight. You got to stop it, now. Eat something, or take some of the pills—you want me to read to you? 'Cause Beth and Laura are coming and—we can't blow it.

JOEL & GHOST *(GHOST, at JOEL's side, moves exactly as JOEL moves. This begins a kind of dance with JOEL and the GHOST, as JOEL moves around and gestures and the GHOST moves exactly as he does. JOEL seems to be re-living this scene with BETH).* Beth and I

JOEL. were

JOEL & GHOST. in her room,

JOEL. and she was

JOEL & GHOST. whispering

JOEL. to me, and holding my hand and

JOEL & GHOST. kissing me,

JOEL. and I knew what she wanted—breathing on me, touching me, saying she loved me. And I was thinking

JOEL & GHOST. I did something

JOEL. …and I was afraid I was going to

JOEL & GHOST. tell her.

JOEL. But

GHOST. I couldn't

JOEL. because

GHOST. I

JOEL. knew I would

JOEL & GHOST. hurt her.

JOEL. She wouldn't stop, she

JOEL & GHOST. Tell her—

JOEL. kept whispering.

JOEL & GHOST. Tell her—

JOEL. She

GHOST. Tell her!

JOEL *(breaking away from GHOST)*. I can't. I can't!

LUCAS. You can't what?

GHOST. Tell her.

JOEL. Hurt her.

LUCAS. What do you think you did?

JOEL *(GHOST moves separately from him now)*. But I wanted to ask you if I...

GHOST. Joel Killer. *(He laughs.)*

JOEL *(turning to GHOST, speaking to him)*. That's not funny! Did you think that was funny?

LUCAS. What was funny?

JOEL *(to LUCAS)*. What's my name?

LUCAS. Joel.

GHOST. Killer.

JOEL. My last name.

LUCAS. Miller.

JOEL. Yes, Miller, not Killer. Miller. Do you think Killer is funny? Joel Killer, is that funny?

GHOST. As funny as death.

LUCAS. Joel, you have to relax—now. They'll be here soon. You want me to play some music? You want me to read to you?

JOEL. Yeah, read, will you read to me? That will help.

LUCAS. Yeah. Yeah, if I can see.

JOEL. Yeah, read to me.

GHOST. Yes, read about us; tell the world about us.

LUCAS *(gets book)*. Were you talking about the poem? Is that where you got killer? He kills the albatross? Or were you hearing something? You looked like you might be hearing something. Because your last name is definitely Miller, not Killer. *(Looks at book.)* I can't…I can't see. I can't read. I'm sorry.

JOEL *(standing, reciting to the lake. Gradually he will calm down. The GHOST will gradually withdraw from JOEL)*.

"The ship drove fast, loud roared the blast,
And southward aye we fled.

And now there came both mist and snow, and it grew
   wondrous cold:
And ice, mast-high, came floating by, as green as
   emerald.

At length did dross an albatross, through the fog it
   came;
As if it had been a Christian soul, we hailed it in
   God's name."

(The GHOST exits.)

"And a good south wind sprung up behind; the
   albatross did follow,
And every day, for food or play,
Came to the mariner's hollo!"

(TRISHA enters, stops and listens to JOEL.)

"God save thee, Ancient Mariner!
From the fiends, that plague thee thus!—"
(Bitterly.)

"Why look'st thou so?—with my crossbow
I shot the albatross."
(His calm begins to change to self-disgust.)
"And I had done a hellish thing,
And it would work 'em woe;
For all averred, I had killed the bird
That made the breeze to blow.
Ah wretch! said they, the bird to slay,
That made the breeze to blow!"

TRISHA *(claps).* That was very good, Joel. *(TRISHA, 5'2", brunette, is a physically graceful animated, attractive young woman. She covers her anxiety well, until something breaks through and we see she is uncommonly nervous in social situations.)*

LUCAS. Trisha, you're here. Look, Joel, Trisha's here. We thought your car broke down.

TRISHA. Did you memorize that for English class?

JOEL. No, no, for myself.

TRISHA. Wow.

JOEL. I was hoping you would come. And you look great. Do you want something? We have a table of food, there's drinks in the cooler.

TRISHA. Where is everybody? You said it was going to be a gathering.

JOEL. It's a small gathering, just a few friends. But you're early.

TRISHA. I'm always early. Who else did you invite?

JOEL. People I like, interesting people; talented people. I don't know why Lucas is here. Did you invite him?

TRISHA. Oh, poor Lucas.

JOEL. I saw you in the play and I was impressed. I didn't know you were so talented.

TRISHA. You're so nice. You're the nicest guy in the world. Isn't he, Lucas?

JOEL. I don't know how you can act in front of people. You seem so...I didn't think you were the kind of person who would like that.

TRISHA. It's because I don't have to think about being me? I'm someone else.

LUCAS. Do you know if Laura is coming?

TRISHA. She didn't say anything to me. Is she bringing Randy?

LUCAS. Is she still dating him?

TRISHA. They came to the play together.

(HOLLY enters carrying a guitar, followed by RICK. RICK is obviously a bodybuilder and wears clothes to show himself off. HOLLY has long hair, jeans and a sad smile.)

LUCAS. Holly! And Rick! Look, Joel, Holly—and *Rick*—are here. Isn't that lucky? *(LUCAS' announcing everyone throughout the play is just him having fun and expressing how he feels about each person at that moment.)*

HOLLY. Hi, Joel. *(They all say hello.)* I hope you don't mind that I invited Rick to your party.

RICK. Hey, Joel.

JOEL. I should have thought of it myself. Thanks for coming, Rick. I'm surprised she got you out of the gym.

RICK. She, ah, she can get me to do just about anything these days. She made me go to a seance last night. We talked to some dead people.

LUCAS. What'd you learn?

RICK. My family's always been screwed up—even a hundred years ago.

JOEL. What else did they say?

RICK. I don't know, I fell asleep.

HOLLY. When do you want me to sing, Joel?

JOEL. Soon as you can.

HOLLY. Well, why don't I get settled first, get Stomach here something to eat and myself something to drink. *(Which she does.)*

JOEL. Help yourself.

TRISHA *(to JOEL)*. You didn't know she was bringing Rick?

JOEL. No.

TRISHA. Oh. Should I have brought someone?

JOEL. Not if you didn't want to.

TRISHA *(becoming a little anxious)*. Because I thought, the way you said it? I thought you were inviting me. I mean, you invited me? but I thought—did you invite Beth, too?

JOEL. I invited interesting and talented people. Like you. And Holly. She's going to sing tonight.

TRISHA. Did you want me to do something, like dance or something? Is that why you invited me?

JOEL. I just wanted you to be here.

TRISHA. But *with you*, Joel? or with someone else—are you trying to set me up, maybe with Lucas, or—

JOEL. I just wanted you to be here.

TRISHA. And I just want to know what's happening. I hate it when I don't know what's going on. *(She begins to breathe anxiously.)*

JOEL *(who is himself becoming anxious)*. Why, what's going on?

TRISHA. I don't know!

JOEL. Neither do I. I'm sorry.

TRISHA. Because I didn't drive. My brother dropped me off and won't be back for at least three hours. *(TRISHA walks away to catch her breath.)*

JOEL *(following her)*. I wanted to talk to you.

TRISHA. What about?

JOEL. Where are you going to college?

TRISHA. You could have asked me that at school.

JOEL. Yes, but…

TRISHA. I'm going to State.

JOEL. Are you sure?

TRISHA. Why? What do you mean? What kind of question is that?

JOEL. I'm sorry.

TRISHA. Yes I'm sure. I'm going to State. *(Seeing someone coming.)* Laura. Did you invite her, too?

(LAURA enters carrying a rolled-up poster. TRISHA uses this moment to move farther away.)

JOEL *(to TRISHA)*. No, Lucas. Lucas invited her.

LAURA. Hey, everybody!

LUCAS. Laura! Look, Joel, it's Laura. *(Everyone says hello, except TRISHA.)*

LAURA. I heard there was a PARTY. *(She pops a streamer. Everyone cheers, except TRISHA.)* Lucas?

LUCAS. Yes, Laura?

LAURA. Although I don't know you very well, I do see that you have an eye for physical beauty.

RICK. Oh, yeah.

LAURA. After all, you said I had the prettiest smile, the best hair, the sexiest walk—

JOEL. He says that, I've heard him.

LAURA. —the same things you said to Juanita Marales last week. *(She swats LUCAS with poster.)*

RICK. You shouldn't do that, man. You gotta know that girls tell each other everything. They put it on the net every night in some secret female website.

LAURA. And you know that we're making a cheesy calendar as part of yearbook this year, with seductive pictures of, well, me, and some other seniors, and so I blew one up because I want you to know aaalllll about me. Just please don't ever show this to my parents. My mother would die. *(She gives it to him, he unfurls it, turns it away from everyone else, looks at it.)*

LUCAS. Oh, baby. I can't believe the school would let you put this on the calendar.

LAURA. They said it revealed too much; they won't let us use it.

HOLLY. Well, let us see. Rick, here, is panting like a dog.

RICK. Yeah, I'm panting like a dog *(He pants.)*

LUCAS *(hugging poster)*. I don't know; this is an intimate moment for me.

RICK. Show us the damn picture, man! *(He turns it around. It is a large, bathing-suit, beefcake, pumped-up portrait of an oiled-down and grimacing RICK. They burst out laughing.)*

HOLLY. Is that...?

LUCAS. It's Rick!

RICK. That came out beautiful, man. Look at those pecs.

HOLLY. Do you want us to leave so you and the picture can be alone?

RICK. Can I have that?

LUCAS. It's mine.

RICK. You want it? Because if you do, I'm going home.

LUCAS *(giving it to RICK).* I wouldn't dream of separating you from your loved one.

RICK *(to HOLLY).* I want you to know I got something more than brains *(He gives it to her.)*

HOLLY. Oh, Rocko, it's never been about your brains.

LUCAS *(to LAURA. The others move to the picnic table).* So, you came.

LAURA. Yeah; my mother wants our house painted.

LUCAS. Ah.

LAURA. I told you I'd come.

LUCAS. Yeah, but… You look…better than you do on that poster.

LAURA. I'm glad.

LUCAS. You came!

LAURA. Yes! I wanted to talk to you.

LUCAS. What about? *(Her cell phone rings. She takes it from her purse and answers it.)*

LAURA. Hello?… *(She turns away from LUCAS.)* Hi, sweetheart.

LUCAS. "Hi, sweetheart."

RICK. She talking to Randy?

LUCAS. Yeah.

LAURA. Yeah, it's beautiful here. The sky is so clear you can see Arcturus, already…

RICK. Take her phone away, man.

HOLLY. Rick!

RICK. What?

HOLLY. Shut your mouth.

RICK *(firmly, positively; she's always right)*. OK.

HOLLY. Bring my guitar over here.

RICK *(firmly, positively)*. OK. *(He does. She will take guitar out of case during the following.)*

LAURA. I don't know… But I just got here… I'll call you later…I can't talk right now… Nobody. *(LUCAS mouths "nobody," moves away. LAURA doesn't see this.)* Look, I'll call you later. In an hour… I promise. Bye sweetheart. *(She hangs up, turns, sees LUCAS has moved. She moves to table to get something to drink as JOEL moves to TRISHA.)*

TRISHA *(to herself. There are two personalities speaking here. One is the "normal" TRISHA, usually more anxious, and the other is an "ideal" Elizabeth, taller, stronger, more socially aware, more beautiful. TRISHA becomes one then the other quickly as they converse. The first voice is soothing, the second is anxious)*. It's all right. It's a beautiful night and no one really cares… But I thought… I know what you thought and I'm sorry… I thought he asked me because… Let me help you, tonight. I feel beautiful out here. I'll help you get through without… Is Joel coming over here? Oh, God. *(She sees him coming, stops talking. He carries a soda, gives it to her.)*

JOEL. I've watched you in school, did you know that?

TRISHA. Yes; you've been staring at me. It's why I thought you asked me here, tonight.

JOEL. And I've seen you at the hospital.

TRISHA *(for a moment, this stops her)*. Everyone knows I was in the hospital, Joel. Just like everybody knows you were at a clinic for a week.

JOEL. Do you... *(He goes towards her, she backs up.)*

TRISHA. What do you want? *(He reaches out and touches her forehead. He puts his other hand on the back of her head. She begins to breathe nervously.)* Let me go.

JOEL. Do you get headaches, and feel like your head is swelling up, right here?

TRISHA *(breathing anxiously, trying to control herself)*. No.

JOEL. And that if it doesn't stop, your head will split open?

TRISHA. No.

JOEL *(greatly relieved, he lets her go)*. Good, good. Good.

TRISHA *(moves away, but turns back, calms down some, feeling safer with distance between them)*. Is this why you invited me? You wanted to talk to me?

JOEL. Were *you tested*?

TRISHA. You mean, like X-rays? *(He indicates yes.)* EKGs, MRIs—

JOEL. I've had all that.

TRISHA. Ultrasounds—

JOEL. And you hear things.

TRISHA *(shocked, she takes this in. After a moment)*. I don't know if I want to talk about this stuff? I just got here, and it's a party, isn't it?

JOEL. Do you hear things?

TRISHA. Do you hear things, Joel?

JOEL. Do they help you?

TRISHA. What do you hear?

JOEL. Do they help you? *(She considers a moment. More vulnerably:)* Or do they…

TRISHA *(seeing his distress, and that this is about him, not her. This is something familiar to her)*. I needed them and so just when I did? They came to help me. Now they all argue. And they…want me to…do things?…like, maybe, things…I don't want to do.

JOEL. You take medication?

TRISHA. I couldn't live my life being paranoid all the time, because if I did it would control me. Then it wouldn't be me, anymore, just this walking…goo of problems. So I take medication.

JOEL. And you're going to college.

TRISHA. Yes I am.

JOEL. And live in the dorm?

TRISHA. There are too many people in the dorm—so even though I can't afford it? I'm going to live in an apartment.

JOEL. Thanks. Thanks for talking to me.

TRISHA. Sure.

JOEL. I'm going to school, too.

TRISHA. Of course, you're one of the smartest guys in school.

JOEL. I want to live in an apartment, too. Lucas and I are getting an apartment. *(JOEL and TRISHA sit together.)*

LAURA *(moving to LUCAS)*. Sorry. Randy's a little nervous about me being here. He doesn't understand why I came.

LUCAS. Why did you come?

LAURA. Why do you stare at me in school?

LUCAS. I'm not telling you anything. There are too many sticks laying around this beach.

LAURA. You're weird. You are so strange.

LUCAS. You like weird?

LAURA. No.

LUCAS. Does it interest you?

LAURA. No.

LUCAS. You want to be college roommates?

LAURA. No!

LUCAS. The only thing weird about Randy is that there is nothing weird about him.

LAURA. That's right. We're going to State together. Besides, Trisha there is who I think you want.

LUCAS. Maybe last year, but not now.

LAURA. Did you invite her, too?

LUCAS. In a fit of madness, my friend Joel invited three women, including the sexy but at the moment, confused Trisha. *(Beat. Suddenly with a lot more energy and drive. And loud enough for all on the beach to hear. They all turn to him and listen.)* I can't help it. You come into psychology class, looking like that, *(Painfully.)* wa, waaaalllking like that, and you're smarter than I am, and you're saying that stuff about "It's important to take responsibility for your dreams, not just blame the world when they don't come true." and "I think it's as important to decide who you want to be as it is where you came from." I hate that. It makes me want to talk to you. You know that everything is much deeper, motivations and goals, the reasons why we do things. You don't seem afraid to ask yourself those questions. I hate that. It makes me want to touch you. You're going to State, too, and you love scuba diving.

LAURA. Do you dive?

LUCAS. I love to dive. I love a lot of things I've never done. I think I'm going to go to college with you and concerts with you and plays with you and read books with you and take psychology classes with you and— what's your major?

LAURA. Anthropology.

LUCAS. Is that saying you're sorry to people? *(Saying it slowly.)* Anthropology.

LAURA. What are you talking about?

LUCAS. You asked me why I stare at you in school.

LAURA. Yeah.

LUCAS. I don't want to waste my time anymore. And if I'm with you, I don't think I ever will. *(After a moment, she stands up.)* Are you going to beat me with a stick?

LAURA. I can't sit here with you right now *(She walks toward the others.)*

LUCAS. Well done, boy. Was it something I said? Maybe everything I said? I told you to talk to her like she's smart, not like you like her. Give me a stick I'll beat myself.

(BETH enters. BETH is a young woman with multiple presentations. She's tough, experienced in the world for her young years, smart in school, and socially an outcast. She's direct, honest, has a loud laugh, and a warm, vulnerable heart.)

BETH. Hi! *(Greetings from everyone. TRISHA stands, moves from JOEL.)*

LUCAS. Beth. Look, Joel, it's Beth. It's going to be a great night. *(BETH and JOEL meet, but do not embrace.)*

TRISHA. Hi, Beth.

BETH. Hello, Trisha. *(Taking JOEL by the arm.)* Can I talk to you?

RICK. Ooo, look out. I heard she's mad at you.

JOEL. Holly, would you sing now?

HOLLY. Sure. *(BETH and JOEL begin to move away from others.)*

RICK *(to JOEL)*. Call me if you need my help.

HOLLY. Rocko!

RICK. Yeah?

HOLLY. Leave them alone.

RICK. I was trying to—

HOLLY. Don't explain yourself.

RICK *(firmly, positively, HOLLY is always right)*. Sorry.

(The DEMON enters, heading straight for JOEL. The DEMON is not human. He wears a dark, painted leotard and tights, with muted designs that move onto his head, hands and feet. His face is pale and his hair is swept back. He moves with the alacrity and sharp focus of a threatened animal.)

DEMON. You know why she's here.

(JOEL veers himself and BETH away. The GHOST enters, moves in their path.)

GHOST. You're going to tell her.

JOEL. Holly!

HOLLY. Yeah?

DEMON. I'll help you.

JOEL. Are you ready?

HOLLY. All set.

GHOST. Tell her.

JOEL. Then sing now. *(She begins intro to "Dreams.")*

BETH. Did you invite Trisha?

DEMON. Get her away from me—

JOEL *(pulling BETH back toward HOLLY and RICK)*. Come on, I want to hear Holly sing.

BETH. But we have to talk.

DEMON. —or she's next.

JOEL. Holly's going to sing. I don't want to be rude.

GHOST. Coward.

HOLLY. I just finished writing this. It's called: "Dreams." And I dedicate it to Rick. *(Applause and cheers, as JOEL sits near HOLLY.)*

LUCAS. Rick! Rick!

(HOLLY sings "Dreams." JOEL tries to calm down, the music helps him relax. TRISHA separates from the others and, to amuse herself, dances off and on to the music. Her dancing comes from both musical plays and classes.)

HOLLY.
> **IT'S SAID IF YOU CAN DREAM IT**
> **YOU CAN MAKE IT REAL.**
> **LIFE AS YOU PERCEIVE IT**
> **HAS ITS OWN APPEAL.**
> **I HAVE NO ILLUSIONS**
> **OF A FUTURE IN THIS PLACE.**

(DEMON recedes into the background, squats on the ground, staring at JOEL; GHOST lies down in an awkward, "murdered" position. JOEL watches them.)

**I WON'T TRADE MY TOMORROWS
FOR YOUR SWEET AND SMILING FACE.
AND I'M FEELING LIKE A DANCER
WHO IS RUNNING OUT OF SPACE.
'CAUSE I WON'T GIVE UP ON MY DREAMS...**

(GHOST and DEMON remain in the background. At this point in the song, BETH gently pulls JOEL far away from HOLLY again. The following occurs during song; HOLLY sings quieter. JOEL will glance at VOICES during the following.)

BETH *(softer)*. Are you in a different mood tonight?

JOEL. Most of the time.

BETH *(less angry, more needing answers)*. Saturday upset me. I was pissed. And extremely disappointed. Were you mad at me? Is that why you just left like that?

JOEL. I'm sorry, Beth. But I did tell you I was getting a headache.

BETH. You said you were depressed.

JOEL. Yeah.

BETH. But, Joel, there was only you and me there. For hours. If you were getting depressed, then I was doing something to upset you.

JOEL. No you weren't. You were great.

BETH. What happened? You kissed me, I felt you loved me, again—

JOEL. Yeah.

BETH. —like last summer.

JOEL. Yeah!

BETH. —You made me laugh.

JOEL. I started getting a headache. *(The DEMON rises, watches from a distance. JOEL sees DEMON rising, starts to move back.)* Let's just listen—

BETH *(stopping them).* How could I tell, Joel? I have been having an extremely hard time telling if you are mad or upset, depressed or thinking or what! I realize that that is the way you react when one of those moods hits you, but what do I do?

JOEL. I asked you to sing.

BETH. Were you serious? I didn't think you were serious; asking me to sing to you, *right then.* Were you? *(JOEL sees the GHOST start to rise, and the DEMON moving toward him.)*

JOEL. It would have made me feel better.

BETH. Did you get mad at me because I didn't?

JOEL. I didn't get mad at you! I got a headache! And I want to hear this song.

(He moves back to HOLLY, sits. DEMON squats again, GHOST lies back down. As HOLLY sings louder again, JOEL focuses on her.)

HOLLY.
> **THE VOICE WAS MY TOMORROWS**
> **THAT I HAD LOCKED INSIDE.**
> **SINGING, NEVER WILL WE EVER, EVER BE**
> **DENIED.**
>
> **'CAUSE I WON'T GIVE UP ON MY DREAMS.**
> **NO, I WON'T GIVE UP ON MY DREAMS**
> **YOU SAY "YOU'RE OUT OF YOUR MIND.**
> **TO LEAVE IT ALL BEHIND."**
> **BUT I WON'T GIVE UP ON MY DREAMS.**

    OOO, OOO, OOO, WON'T GIVE UP ON MY
      DREAMS.
    OOO, OOO, OOO, WON'T GIVE UP ON MY
      DREAMS.

(All clap and cheer.)

RICK *(suddenly on his knees in great pain, crawling to HOLLY)*. Ah! You can't go to Eastern without me. Who's going to sing to me? Some fullback?

HOLLY. Are you sure you want our friends to see this side of you?

TRISHA/LUCAS. More, more./Go, Rick, go!

RICK. Come with me to Western like we planned. You got accepted.

LUCAS/TRISHA. Yeah!/Western!

HOLLY. I told you: Eastern has a better music program.

RICK. I'll go to seances. I'll talk to dead people. I'll become a Taurus…with my moon rising.

LUCAS. Oh, no, I can see that.

HOLLY. Rick, we have a seventh house transit going on, you know that.

RICK. Yeah.

LUCAS. What?

HOLLY. It feels exciting, it feels magical, but our charts don't have a longevity schedule in them.

RICK. But if I don't understand that stuff, it shouldn't work on me, right?

LAURA & BETH. Right.

LUCAS & TRISHA. That's right.

HOLLY. You're having the sun rise on your Venus, but I'm not. It's not in my chart. I showed you.

GROUP. Awwww, Riiiicckkk.

RICK. If I can tackle fullbacks, I can rip up those damn charts.

LUCAS. But don't anybody touch that poster.

HOLLY. There will never be another Rocko in my life.

RICK. What does that mean?

HOLLY. You're...one of a million.

RICK. Then come with me to Western. No one tells me what to do better than you.

HOLLY. My sweet Rocko.

LUCAS. Rick, sometime I have to talk to you about...stuff.

(BETH is pulling JOEL away again. GHOST rises, DEMON rises.)

JOEL. What?

BETH. I want to finish talking to you. *(DEMON and GHOST move toward JOEL.)*

GHOST. You can't run away anymore.

JOEL. But we talked, already.

GHOST. It's time, Joel, it's your time.

BETH. I want to tell you what I've been thinking.

GHOST. Time to tell her.

DEMON. If she stays too close—

JOEL. But everything is...

DEMON. The death-fires will burn her.

JOEL. ...all right, now.

DEMON. They're burning all around you.

JOEL *(looking around quietly)*. Burning...

BETH. What?

JOEL. Holly, will you sing, again?

HOLLY. Give me a few minutes. I got my sad Rocko here.

JOEL. As soon as you can, all right?

HOLLY. All right.

GHOST. I was like her. And the others. Remember? Normal. Healthy.

JOEL *(to GHOST)*. I'm sorry.

GHOST. Remember?

BETH. For what?

JOEL. I remember.

GHOST. Like a child.

BETH. What do you remember? Why are you sorry?

JOEL *(to BETH)*. What do you want to say?

DEMON *(laughing)*. Listen to this!

BETH. When I first started liking you, there were a lot of things in our way—like my reputation. But still I wanted to see you. So I started to dress better and clean up my act for what seemed like the fifty billionth time, but somehow I knew that this time it would work. Instead of "Gimme drugs! Gimme drugs!" I'm saying "Gimme Joel! Gimme Joel!"

GHOST *(whispering)*. Tell her, tell her—

BETH. And then, when I went three weeks without being grounded for life, again, my parents even liked you.

GHOST. Tell her what you did to me.

BETH. They're terrified we're going to break up and I'll go back to the way I was.

GHOST. You picked up the knife—

BETH. It's taken me about four years to go through all the garbage to finally find a person like you.

GHOST. You came up behind me—

BETH. And if we break up now, I'm not sure what will happen to my mental health.

JOEL. Your mental health?

DEMON *(laughing)*. Your mental health.

BETH. And then you, you made this dream with me, about college and getting married and a family.

DEMON. More jokes.

JOEL. That's right.

BETH. I hadn't thought about that before; not really, not for me.

JOEL. That's what I want, with you.

DEMON. You can't go to college. You will always stay because here is where the body is. Unless you listen to me.

BETH. But I can't do this by myself; you HAVE to talk to me.

GHOST. You will never leave. You will die here like me. You'll rot under the sand.

BETH. Because, because Freebe's calling, again, and I didn't know what was wrong with us, I almost went out with him last night—you have to stop me, Joel, or I'll just go. I will, I'll just go.

JOEL. No.

BETH. Just tell me it's not some other girl. Is it Trisha? Did you invite her because you thought I wouldn't come?

JOEL. Yes I did, but...

DEMON. You see how much she knows? She can read your mind. *(JOEL gets a stabbing pain through his head. He tries not to show it.)*

BETH. What? What is it?

GHOST. You don't deserve her. Look at her; she's good. She'll never go with you. You're not like her, anymore.

JOEL *(another pain. Again he tries to appear calm).* Mmm.

BETH. Joel?

JOEL *(through the pain, trying to stay calm)*. I don't want anyone else. And that dream; it's not going to change for me. No matter what happens.

BETH. Then last Saturday, what was wrong? Were you scared of something?

DEMON. That's enough. You've listened enough. Stop her.

GHOST. She knows you. She can smell you. You foul the air.

BETH. Were you scared of me?

JOEL. Why? Why did you ask me that?

BETH. You looked scared. Were you afraid of what we might do?

DEMON. You stop her now or I'll burn her.

BETH. Don't you want...didn't you want to...I thought you wanted...

JOEL. I was afraid—

DEMON. NO! *(Gestures at JOEL, who grabs his head in pain.)*

JOEL. Ah! *(LUCAS hears this, watches from a distance.)*

GHOST. Yes, tell her!

BETH. Joel, do you have your medicine here?

JOEL. I was afraid I was going to tell you something—

DEMON. They'll never forgive you—

JOEL. Something I didn't—

DEMON. I'll punish you—

GHOST. You will never laugh again unless you tell her.

DEMON. I'll make you do things you can't imagine.

JOEL. Something I didn't want you to know.

DEMON. Stop this or I'll push your skull apart from the inside. *(He gestures at JOEL, JOEL grabs his head in pain, pounds on his forehead.)*

JOEL. Stop it! Stop it! *(The others see and hear this.)* Lucas! Lucas, come here! Can you come here?

LUCAS. Yeah? *(He moves toward JOEL, who is pounding on his forehead.)*

BETH. Joel, don't, don't, sweetheart.

LUCAS. Joel, stop it. I'll get your pills.

JOEL. Do you see this? *(LUCAS moves to picnic table to get a drink and tablets. JOEL starts to move toward LUCAS, the GHOST cuts him off.)*

GHOST. You coward, you can't run from me. I can follow you everywhere, now. I'm with you forever. *(JOEL moves around him.)*

DEMON *(following JOEL; fearful)*. Lie to them like you always do; they don't know who you are. I'll help you.

LUCAS *(moving to JOEL with drink and pills)*. What is it?

JOEL. My head—it's swelling. I can't stop it. Can't you see?

LUCAS. I can't see anything.

DEMON. Get out of this now!

JOEL & GHOST *(suddenly reciting. The GHOST, side by side with JOEL, again moves exactly like JOEL. It's a dance, as JOEL acts out the poem dramatically, energetically. This time, the poem seems to give JOEL a strength; he becomes less and less frantic as the poem goes on, the pain in his head disappears. The others watch in puzzlement)*.

    "And I had done a hellish thing,

    And it would work 'em woe;

    For all averred, I had killed the bird..."

GHOST. "That made breeze to blow."

JOEL. "The very deep did rot: O Christ!"

JOEL & GHOST. "That ever this should be!"

JOEL. "Yea, slimy things did crawl
     With legs upon the slimy sea."
JOEL, GHOST & DEMON.
     "About, about, in reel and rout
     The death-fires danced at night;"
JOEL & DEMON. "The water, like a witch's oils,"
JOEL, GHOST & DEMON. "Burnt green and blue and
     white."
DEMON. Death-fires will burn them all. Reel and rout
     them all! They'll all burn in your fire!
JOEL *(to LUCAS, without pain, determined)*. You told me
     if I asked you something you'd tell me the truth.
LUCAS. Take these.
JOEL *(taking them)*. Did I do something that I've forgotten?
LUCAS. It's all right, Joel, just relax.
JOEL. Something horrible?
BETH. What do you think you've done?
LUCAS. Take a walk with me and you can relax. You're
     just having another headache.
DEMON. I told you to stop this! *(Gestures toward JOEL.)*
JOEL *(this time, he only feels a slight jab)*. Because I'm
     being punished. I killed someone; you know I did. *(The
     VOICES stop moving. Silence.)*
GHOST. There.
JOEL *(relieved)*. There... There...I told you. *(He relaxes.)*
LUCAS. Joel...Joel, this is like the other stuff. It didn't
     happen.
HOLLY. Are you kidding? You're kidding, aren't you. Is
     this some weird party game?
JOEL. I killed someone and buried him out here on the
     beach.
GHOST. Now you'll never be the same.

LUCAS. You didn't kill anybody. Look at me. You didn't kill anybody.

TRISHA *(laughs quietly)*. Joel...

JOEL. You know where he is; you're going to dig him up. I just can't figure out why you're taking so long.

DEMON. I told you. Look at their faces. They see you, now. *(JOEL does. He begins to lose his strength.)*

GHOST. You cannot kill and not die, too.

DEMON *(fearful)*. What are you going to do?

GHOST. You will rot under the sand like me. They will go without you.

TRISHA. Is that what your voices are telling you?

GHOST. Who are you?

BETH. Voices? What voices?

GHOST. Killer.

JOEL. What's my last name?

LUCAS. Miller!

GHOST, DEMON & JOEL. Miller the Killer.

LUCAS. You didn't kill anybody.

JOEL. Why else would I have to go through this? Why would I be punished like this?

TRISHA. They don't always tell the truth. Joel! They don't always tell the truth.

GHOST & DEMON *(chanting underneath rest of scene)*. Miller the Killer, Miller the Killer—

JOEL. Get out! Get out! *(He screams in pain, falls to his knees, pounds on his forehead with both hands. LUCAS moves behind him, grabs one hand.)* Leave me alone! Leave me alone! Leave me alone!

LUCAS. Stop it, Joel. Joel!

BETH. Joel, stop it!

LUCAS. Rick!

RICK *(grabs the other arm)*. Easy, boy, easy, easy.
GHOST, DEMON & JOEL. Miller the Killer, Miller the Killer! *(Blackout.)*

SCENE II

SCENE: *The scene is set in two places simultaneously: Joel's beach and the day room of a twelve-bed, acute-care adolescent psychiatric ward. Action will pass from one to the other.*

AT RISE: *Lights come up on the day room of the adolescent psych ward. Evening. KATHERINE, an expensively dressed young woman, sits unmoving at a table, in a catatonic state. The look on her face is one of pained, grim determination. JULIE lays on the floor, drawing with crayons on a sketch pad. JULIE's thin and small, and completely vulnerable. Someone has dressed her in a nice dress. On that dress is tied a large bird feather.*

JULIE. The walls will be so high no one can see over them. No one will ever find us. The walls will look like the sky, so no one will even see them. We'll live inside and we'll have peacocks; I know you like peacocks because you like their feathers; blue and green. We'll have a park; our park; with a fountain and a pool, and I'll swim in our pool and no one will hurt me this time. The fountain will look like an angel. I'm ready, now, Jacob. I wasn't before, but now I'm ready and I can show you how to go there with me. But you have to come, now. You have to come soon, so I don't have to go with someone else. *(Turns to KATHERINE.)* Where is Jacob? *(Silence.)* When is he coming?

(KATHERINE remains unmoving. JULIE exits as lights crossfade down on day room and up on Joel's beach. HOLLY is snacking, RICK is pacing. LAURA enters.)

LAURA. Did they get back from the hospital?

HOLLY. Not yet. Did Lucas call you?

LAURA. He doesn't have my number.

RICK. What will they do with him?

LAURA. I guess the doctor will talk to him—I don't know. I've never seen anything like that before.

RICK. Yeah. Me either. I didn't know what to do.

HOLLY *(to LAURA)*. Are you going to wait?

LAURA. That's what Lucas wanted.

RICK. Are we waiting?

HOLLY. Yes.

RICK. For a while?

HOLLY. Yeah.

RICK. OK. *(That settled, RICK does some thinking.)*

HOLLY. Joel was always a little strange—which is one of the reasons I like him—but, wow, he was out there.

LAURA. This must be why Joel went to that clinic.

HOLLY. They don't seem to have helped him.

RICK. I'll give you my car!

HOLLY. Your Jeep?

RICK. Yeah, baby!

HOLLY. For what?

RICK. Go to Western with me. I can't go to Eastern, their football program sucks!

HOLLY. We're talking about Joel, now.

RICK. I know, but no one here knows anything. So we're just waiting. I need something to do while I'm waiting. I hate waiting.

HOLLY. I want to wait until we hear something.

RICK. OK. I'm waiting. And I won't talk if we're talking about Joel.

HOLLY. All right.

LAURA *(as she moves to sit by herself)*. Lucas promised he'd come back as soon as he could. *(Pause. RICK looks from one to the other.)*

RICK *(seeing no one is talking about JOEL)*. Why you doing this to me? I know you like me. And you gotta love me. So what's the problem?

HOLLY. Rocko, there's no problem; you're not a problem.

RICK. If there's no problem, what's the problem?

HOLLY. I changed. Last year I wanted to be a teacher and Western's teaching program would have been fine. But now I want to play music.

RICK. You can play music anywhere.

HOLLY. They have the right contacts at Eastern.

RICK. Would you still see me if I went there?

HOLLY. You can't give up football for me.

RICK. We're perfect. We're just perfect together.

HOLLY. You should feel lucky—I do. We're not guaranteed to have this kind of relationship in this lifetime. But you can't trust it to last forever.

RICK. Damn it! What am I going to do?

HOLLY. I know what you'll do.

RICK. Yeah, I'm going to eat. I'm going to sit in my room and I'm going to eat. And I'm going to miss you. Then I'm going to eat some more, and I'm going to miss you some more. And then I'm going to eat some more. And

then I'm going to start looking like I used to—Fatboy.
Truckbutt. And then I'm going to have to drive all
across the state, and find you.

HOLLY. And then what?

RICK. Well, yeah, we'll, yeah, ah, of course, I think you're
happy to see me. Are you?

HOLLY. Always. Then you're going to have to go practice
the next day.

RICK. Yeah, I'll commute.

HOLLY. Two hundred and fifty miles?

RICK. So I need my Jeep after all. I can't give it to you.

HOLLY. Come here.

*(He does, she kisses him. LUCAS and BETH enter
beach.)*

LUCAS. Hey, thanks for waiting.

LAURA. What happened?

LUCAS. His mother took him into the doctor's office and
after about half an hour they took him into the main
building.

BETH. We walked with him down a hall and then a nurse
took him inside the ward and locked the door.

LUCAS. They said we couldn't visit for three days.

HOLLY. How long is he going to be there?

BETH. They didn't know.

RICK. What did they say was wrong with him?

BETH. They didn't tell us anything.

LUCAS. They won't even let me talk to him for three
days.

BETH. What's wrong with him, Lucas?

LUCAS. I don't know. Something in his brain.

BETH. Where did all those things come from he was saying?

LUCAS. I don't know.

BETH. He believed what he was saying.

LUCAS. None of it's true.

BETH. No, it can't be. None of that can be true. Can it?

LUCAS. No. He's said things like that before, only not so bad.

BETH. He scared me. I didn't know what to do. I couldn't believe it. Joel...?

(Lights crossfade down on beach, up on day room. KATHERINE is still sitting in same position, JULIE is gone. TOM enters with JOEL, giving him a tour of the ward. JOEL is subdued, tranquilized; TOM is nicely dressed, bright and helpful.)

TOM. This is the day room. When you're not in therapy or group or you're tired of being in your room, you can hang out in here. Games, TV, Katherine. Hi, Katherine. *(No response, of course.)* She's not moving much, lately.

(COBY enters behind TOM, gooses him.)

COBY. Tom! Just trying to take that long stick out of your butt. *(COBY is a big girl, loud and direct. She wears a T-shirt with the sleeves ripped out, tight, old jeans and boots. She also wears a large bandage on one of her upper arms.)*

TOM. This is Coby; she's impossible to ignore. Coby, Joel.

COBY. Hey, welcome to where it isn't. *(Shaking his hand.)* Don't tell anyone anything you don't want everyone to know. *(Aside to JOEL.)* You smuggle in any cigarettes?

JOEL. No.

COBY. Damn, you could go crazy in here waiting for one. Well, Katherine, back to the game.

TOM. Chess, with a catatonic?

COBY *(sitting at chessboard in front of KATHERINE).* Have you decided on your next move, Princess?

TOM. Do you think that's a fair game?

COBY. As fair as any in life, Tom. *(Moving KATHERINE's piece.)* You want to move your knight here, Princess? What a darlin' move. And this is my move. *(She moves her piece onto the same square, pounds on KATHERINE's piece.)* Die! Die! Die! Die! *(She throws piece onto floor. Sweetly.)* Sorry, sweetheart. Your knight died.

TOM. Isn't that a little cruel?

COBY. She'll remember this later when she starts moving again. Then it'll really piss her off. This time I want her to have a reason to be mad at me and squeal on me about hoardin' food in my room. *(To KATHERINE.)* And you can tell the nurses, again, where I hide my cigarettes, Princess. *(To TRISHA.)* She'll love it.

TOM. Why don't you take whatever problem you're having to group and leave her alone.

COBY. Hey, we're supposed to relate. I'm relating.

TOM. But in positive ways.

COBY. It's positive! I'm winning!

(JULIE enters.)

JULIE *(to TOM)*. I want to see Jacob.

TOM. He's no longer living, Julie.

JULIE. No longer living? *(She exits.)*

TOM. That was Julie.

JOEL. Is this going to help me?

TOM. Come on, I'll show you the rec room and my favorite room, the kitchen. *(They exit.)*

COBY *(quickly turning back to chessboard)*. Did you move somethin' while my back was turned? *(She looks at KATHERINE. No response. Sings.)* "She'll be coming 'round the mountain when she comes—" *(Indicates for KATHERINE to sing line. No response.)* "She'll be coming 'round the mountain when she comes—" *(Again indicating for KATHERINE to sing. No response. Looking into KATHERINE's eyes.)* Damn, something must have happened to you, girl. Come on, it's just you and me, now. What was it? *(No response.)* Mira, chica, quiero ayudarte!* What has hurt you? *(No response.)* Your move. *(Looks at board.)* Your other knight…? *(She holds piece up, rides it in the air.)* Look at him ride so proud and perfect…just like you…pretty and proud and perfect…here? Perfect. *(She picks up her queen.)* This is my queen. *(She pounds it on KATHERINE's knight.)* Boom!!! Boom!!! DIE!!! DIE!!! *(She throws it away. Sweetly.)* All your knights are gone. Sometimes, things happen to you you can't believe. And then you ain't got no more knights… Now what are you going to do? Freeze up and stop the world. That's a plan I guess. For a while.

(TRISHA enters day room.)

---

* Look girl, I want to help you.

TRISHA. Of course— Playing chess with a catatonic?

COBY. Artiste! Look, Katherine, it's Trisha the Artiste! *(TRISHA and COBY embrace.)* Hey, you're just visitin', right?

TRISHA. Oh, yeah, I'm fine.

COBY. How'd you know I was in?

TRISHA. I just guessed.

COBY. Lucky guess. I get out this weekend. We got to get together!

TRISHA *(taking COBY's arm, referring to the bandage)*. What did you do?

COBY. Ah, I was doin' great, then Ronnie jumped on the Harley and headed out West without me. Broke our dreams.

TRISHA. This wasn't going to happen again.

COBY. Yeah, I forgot everything I knew. Went back to what I was.

TRISHA. We can't do that.

COBY. It's good to see you! This place is borin' without you dancin' in the halls and Katherine not screamin' at everybody, yet. How you doin'? You're lookin' great!

TRISHA. I'm going to college next year.

COBY. Aw, man, that's hot. Damn, girl, goin' to college! You goin' in art?

TRISHA. Yeah.

COBY. Yeah, you're an artist, Trisha! That's you! I knew you'd move ahead! Hey, Katherine, Trisha's goin' to college! What are you goin' to do when you get off that royal butt of yours? You dropped out of high school, Princess. *(Back to TRISHA.)* She'll tell me later.

(JOEL and TOM walk back in. DYING GIRL, one of JOEL's VOICES, enters with them. She is not speaking, but she is there, and JOEL knows she is. She moves through the room, checking it and the people out. DYING GIRL is strong, womanly, elegant and—surprisingly—capable of real warmth and compassion. She's dressed in normal, lovely clothes and has a deep, open wound on her forehead. Her skin is pale. JOEL sees TRISHA, but he's not sure if she's there or not.)

TOM. If there's anything you want, talk to your nurse. You always have one assigned to you. But you can talk to any of the nurses. They're all nice.

(During the following, until she speaks, DYING GIRL kneels, carefully touches her head with her handkerchief, looks at it to see if there is fresh blood on it—there is. She touches it to her head again, to remove the blood, then ritualistically folds her handkerchief, puts it away.)

TRISHA *(to COBY)*. I'll be back.

TOM. Will you be all right?

JOEL. Yeah. *(TRISHA steps toward JOEL. JOEL looks to TOM, then back at TRISHA.)*

TRISHA. I'm really here, if that's what you're thinking.

JOEL *(quite subdued, tranquilized)*. Hey, Trisha. How did you get in?

TRISHA. I know people here. Hi, I'm Trisha.

TOM. I'm Tom. Pleased to meet you. You know Joel?

TRISHA. Yeah, he invited me to his party, tonight.

TOM. Oh, that's nice. *(He sits on couch, reads.)*

DYING GIRL *(rising)*. Look at me.

JOEL *(to TRISHA)*. Why are you here?

TRISHA To see how you're doing?

DYING GIRL. Look at me. Look at what you've done.

JOEL. I don't know if I should be here.

TRISHA. I think you should, even though it's hard—especially at first. And then? You'll get some answers and you'll start to understand things because right now, I don't think anything is making sense to you.

JOEL. Yeah.

DYING GIRL. Look at me.

JOEL. I see you! What do you want me to do?!

DYING GIRL. Don't give up on me. Don't leave me to die.

JOEL. How can I leave you? You are always here!

TRISHA. And I wanted to tell you: it gets better.

JOEL. What? Oh. Thanks.

DEMON *(suddenly appearing)*. She wants to see you, to tell the others. The doctors sent her.

JOEL *(to DEMON)*. No they didn't. Leave her alone.

DYING GIRL. Listen to her. She can help you.

DEMON *(referring to DYING GIRL)*. Let this one die, like the others. You will never go with her.

TRISHA. Do you know what I just said?

JOEL. When?

TRISHA. Just a minute ago?

JOEL. You told me it gets better.

DEMON *(referring to TRISHA)*. If she stays we'll hurt her.

JOEL *(to TRISHA)*. I think you'd better go.

TRISHA. Is there anything you want me to tell Beth and Lucas?

JOEL. Tell them it gets better.

TRISHA. I'm going to visit with my friend Coby, and then? if you want to talk to me, again, just tell me.

JOEL. I want to see—

DYING GIRL. Don't forget me. You did this.

JOEL. I want to see—

DYING GIRL. If you let me die, you will die. You know that.

JOEL. Yes I know!

TRISHA. You want to see Beth?

JOEL. Beth?

TRISHA. You said you wanted to see…?

JOEL. Lucas. Tell Lucas I have to talk to him.

DEMON. He won't come. He knows what you did. He's afraid of you.

TRISHA. I'll tell him to come as soon as he can. *(She returns to COBY. JOEL takes DYING GIRL's hand, leads her to a place, sits with her. Then he takes her handkerchief and carefully blots the blood on her forehead.)*

COBY. New guy.

TRISHA. Yeah.

(Lights fade on day room, up on beach. LUCAS talks to LAURA. HOLLY sits near RICK, as she STRUMS GUITAR under the scene. BETH sits off alone.)

LAURA. What's your major going to be?

LUCAS. My secret major, which I don't tell anybody, is Major League. I want to pitch. I just don't know if I'm good enough. But otherwise, psychology.

LAURA. What do you want to do in psychology?

LUCAS. Understand Joel. I don't know. Do you know what you want to do?

LAURA. I like cultural anthropology; but I'd love to go out on some paleolithic digs. I like geology. And astronomy. I want to take courses in everything. I'll probably be in college for the next twenty years. So I guess I don't know either.

LUCAS. You say the sexiest things.

LAURA. What sexy things?

LUCAS. "I love cultural anthropology. And geology. And astronomy. I want to take courses in everything. I'd love to go out on some paleolithic digs."

LAURA *(smiles at him)*. What did you mean when you said you didn't want to waste your time anymore?

LUCAS. I have to start making sense of this stuff, like Joel and, and you. I feel stupid. If I understood more I'd be…stronger. I'd be able to help him more—and myself. And I'd be able to…maybe, see you. And I want something to be excited about; really excited about. I love baseball, but…there's more; I know there's a lot more. You're excited about so much.

(He slowly moves toward her. She doesn't know exactly what he's doing. He slowly puts his arms around her. She goes with this, slowly. Then he hugs her, she responds and they stand together. Lights fade on beach, up on day room. TRISHA is gone. Everyone else is as we left them except the DEMON squats some distance from JOEL. DEMON will keep his distance throughout the scene, pushed away and somewhat subdued by JOEL's meds. JULIE reenters. She sees JOEL for the first time.)

JULIE *(brightly. She has a brilliant smile)*. There. There you are! *(She goes to JOEL, hugs him and holds on.)*

You're finally here. Now I don't ever have to go back to where I was.

TOM. Wow. She seems to like you.

JULIE. I knew you'd come if I waited here.

TOM. Does she know you?

JOEL. No. What do I do?

TOM. She doesn't touch anyone.

COBY. She doesn't let anyone touch her. Are you sure you don't know her?

JOEL. I don't think so.

TOM. Oh, do you have periods of amnesia?

JOEL. Not that I remember.

TOM *(laughing).* Ah, you're clever.

COBY. Hey, that's funny. Thanks for a joke.

JULIE *(still holding onto JOEL).* You don't know me because I'm older. You'll remember soon. And you can't leave, because you're finally here, with me.

JOEL *(to VOICES).* It's all right?

DEMON. It's all right.

DYING GIRL. If you never want to leave here.

JOEL *(carefully puts his arms around her).* Stay. Stay here.

DYING GIRL. You don't know what you're doing.

JULIE. I know who you are, Jacob. And I know why you're here.

JOEL. My name is Joel.

TOM. Julie, that's not Jacob, his name is Joel.

JOEL. Who's Jacob?

TOM. I think Jacob was a boy she new, once, who died, somehow.

JULIE *(singing his name).* Jaaacoob.

TOM. Julie, I don't think you should be doing this.

DYING GIRL. She won't let me near you.

COBY. Let her alone, narc; let 'em both alone. Let 'em enjoy it while they got it.

TOM. You don't have to let her do that to you, Joel.

COBY. Hey! What did I just tell you!

TOM. "Let her alone, narc; let 'em both alone. Let 'em enjoy it while they got it."

COBY. Yeah, that's right.

TOM. Thanks. I have a good memory.

COBY. Then do it!

DYING GIRL. How can you heal me if you're with her?

TOM. That's not Jacob, that's Joel.

JULIE *(singing the names)*. Jaaccoob, Jooeelll, Jaacooob.

(Lights fade on day room, up on beach. LUCAS lays next to LAURA looking at the night sky. BETH sits apart. RICK and HOLLY are not there.)

LUCAS. Is that the Milky Way?

LAURA. Yeah. We're looking at the spiral, edge on; that's why it looks like that.

LUCAS. How many stars are there?

LAURA. In our galaxy?

LUCAS. Everywhere.

LAURA. Well...If you take a handful of sand *(she does)* you're holding probably 10,000 grains. That's about how many stars we can see with our eyes. But there are more stars than all the grains of sand on all beaches of the earth.

LUCAS. Amazing.

LAURA. What amazes me is how long ago those stars shone like that. We're actually looking back hundreds—sometimes thousands—of years into the past. It's taken the light that long to travel to the earth. And some of those stars we see aren't stars. They're galaxies. Galaxies of stars. Only they're so far away they look like a star. *(He leans over to kiss her.)* What are you doing?

LUCAS. Trying to tell you something.

LAURA. My ear is over here.

LUCAS *(leaning in again)*. Why do you say such romantic things if you don't want me to—

LAURA *(suddenly grabbing the hair on the back of his head, pulling his head away from her, holding it at arm's length)*. Lucas! *(She stares at him for a couple moments, trying to decide what to do. Then she pulls him to her and kisses him. After another couple of moments, her cell phone rings.)* Oh, I forgot to call. *(She answers phone.)*

LUCAS *(quietly, to the heavens)*. Thank you, stars.

LAURA. Hello?... Oh, hi... Yes I am... Yes he is. Just a minute. *(She holds the phone out to LUCAS.)* It's for you.

LUCAS. Randy wants to talk to me already? *(Looking around.)* Where is he, in the bushes?

LAURA. It's Trisha.

LUCAS *(quickly taking phone)*. Hey, Trisha... You did?... They won't even let me talk to him on the phone... yeah, how do I get in?... Katherine?... Katherine Lewis... Right... What about Beth?... All right... Hey, thanks... Bye. *(He gives phone back to LAURA.)* She told me to say I'm the cousin of another patient, and then I can get in to see Joel. Did you drive?

LAURA. Yeah.

LUCAS. Will you give me a lift to the hospital?

LAURA. Now?

LUCAS. Yeah.

(As he moves toward BETH, lights fade on beach, up on the day room. JOEL is sitting on the floor with JULIE. COBY is brushing KATHERINE's hair and TOM reads a book. JOEL continues to be tired and distracted. DYING GIRL and DEMON are near him.)

COBY *(brushing KATHERINE's hair)*. I wish you weren't so damn angry when you come out of it—we could be friends. I know you remember everything later, so you remember this, too: You're a bitch. So you need all the friends you can get. Let go of some of that upbringing of yours and get to know me; you'll be surprised how alike we are.

JOEL. How long have you been here?

JULIE. Four days. Because I knew you were coming. And my doctor says I have to leave here next Wednesday so I have to get ready. And I am, now that you're here.

JOEL. What's my name?

JULIE. Joel.

JOEL. What do you want?

JULIE. Stay with me.

DYING GIRL. Go with me.

JOEL. I'll hurt you.

DYING GIRL. She'll bury our dreams.

JULIE. You wouldn't hurt me.

DYING GIRL. I will.

JULIE. Not like them.

DYING GIRL. Go with me now, like before.

JOEL. Who hurt you?

DYING GIRL. Before you did this to me, or I'll do this to her.

JULIE. I couldn't help it. I didn't know what they wanted. They were all yelling at me. I tried to listen to them, I tried to do what I was supposed to. But….this was me. It was only me. So they hit me, again, like when I was locked in the room.

JOEL. You were locked in a room? *(She indicates yes.)* For how long?

JULIE. Four years. So when they hit me again I asked to come here. To wait for you. And now you're here. So I'm safe. And I can leave, again, with you, but we have to go before next Wednesday. We'll go when you tell me we are going, Jacob. *(Singing word in hopeful desperation.)* Goooiinnng. Gooiinngg.

DYING GIRL. Beth.

JOEL. I have a girlfriend. Her name is Beth. You'll see her someday.

DEMON. Beth is gone. You know she is.

JULIE *(standing up, showing how her body has changed)*. I'm changing. Do you see? I'm older. I feel older, too. I'm all new. It just happened to me. And I'm ready for you, now. We won't go back where we were. We'll go into our dream. *(Back down to him.)* When we were apart all those years, I made a dream with you. And I told it to you, but I wasn't sure you could hear me. If you didn't, I wrote it down for you, Joel. *(She takes out a piece of paper, gives it to him. Sings his name in that hopeful desperation.)* Joooeelll.

DYING GIRL. Beth.

DEMON. Beth is gone.

JOEL. I'm going to college in the fall. With Beth. And Lucas.

DYING GIRL. Yes, "God save thee...from the fiends that plague thee." *(DEMON laughs.)*

JULIE. Now that you are changing and you are with me, again, we are both ready.

JOEL. I'm changing?

DEMON. Coming to me.

JULIE. It's why you're here. You are changing and it was time for you to find me so we can stay together. So you can't go to college with Beth and Lucas.

JOEL. Why did you say that? How can you know?

JULIE *(taking paper from JOEL)*. Let me show you our dream.

DEMON. Listen to her.

DYING GIRL. Burn it, before she burns you.

JULIE *(opens paper, shows him)*. After we die, we'll live inside tall, faraway walls that no one can climb. There will be trees of food inside; and a waterfall with a pool of water.

JOEL. This isn't for me. Why are you—

DEMON. Listen to her or I will twist your brain.

DYING GIRL. Leave her here, get away, let her die alone.

JULIE. We'll make a house near there, with a porch. And we'll have a bird—a peacock! I have a feather; see? And-we-won't-hurt-any-more. But we have to go before five days because that's when they want to bring me to a new home.

JOEL. Why are you saying this to me? Who are you?

DEMON *(twisting JOEL's brain)*. I told you to listen!

JOEL & DYING GIRL *(holding their heads, and groaning)*. Ah! *(JULIE moves from JOEL, curls up in a cor-*

ner in fear. JOEL pounds the floor. COBY wakes up,
TOM lowers book.)

DYING GIRL. Leave him alone!

TOM. Joel?

JOEL. Is she here? Is she telling me these things?

TOM. Julie? Yeah, she's there.

JOEL. What am I suppposed to do? I didn't hurt her. Did
I?

COBY. No. Relax, Joel; Julie just likes you. Enjoy it.

DEMON. Relax, Joel, everything is all right; except you're
not listening! *(Again twisting JOEL's brain. Both JOEL
and DYING GIRL react to this.)*

JOEL *(to VOICES, his fingers shaking on his forehead).*
Leave me alone!

DEMON. I'm trying to help you!

JULIE. What are you thinking? What are you saying?
What are you going to do?... What did I do? Did I do
something? I'll sit here and you tell me. *(She paces anxiously.)* I'll sit here and wait until you tell me. *(She
paces, tugs at herself.)* Do I have to go to a new home
on Wednesday? Is that why you're not talking? Show
me your thoughts. *(Pulling at her arms, then her face
and hair.)* Show me what you are thinking.

DEMON. You see who you are. You're hurting her.

JULIE *(pulling at herself).* A new home. On Wednesday. A
new home.

COBY. Julie. Julie, stop it. Don't hurt yourself, too!
(Taking JULIE's arms in her hands, stopping her.)

DYING GIRL. You see what she is?

JULIE *(panics).* No, let me go!

COBY. That's been done to you, enough.

JULIE. Don't touch me! Let me go. Let me go!

COBY. I will if you won't hurt yourself.

JULIE. Joel, help me. Help me. She'll kill me! Joel! She's killing me!

DEMON. Miller!

TOM. Shall I get her nurse?

DEMON. You help her!

JOEL. Let her go. *(COBY does.)* Come here.

(He puts his arms out and she embraces him. HOLLY's GUITAR is heard in a slow, rhythmic intro to "Over Water." Lights up on beach; lights remain up on day room. HOLLY sits, playing guitar, RICK and BETH sit near her.)

COBY. That is amazing. You got some secret, my friend; I wish I had your talents; I wouldn't be in here.

JULIE. You see, Jacob. It's why you came. You were changing and so you came to find me. And now we can go, together.

HOLLY *(sings "Over Water," quietly, under the lines below. Once she starts singing, DEMON says his line, and action continues over the song).*

OVER WATER,
BEYOND THE BEACH,
PAST THE SUNSET,
BEYOND ITS REACH.

THERE YOUR TROUBLES
ARE NO MORE,
THAN GRAINS OF SAND,
ON SOME DISTANT SHORE.

> **AND NO CREATURE ON THE WATER,**
> **LAND OR SKY,**
> **NO WOMAN, MAN OR CHILD SHALL EVER CRY,**
> **ON THIS SPHERE,**
> **WITHOUT THE WATER CATCHING EVERY**
>   **TEAR.**

DEMON. You see? Doesn't this feel right? Don't you love her?

(TOM relaxes, sits, resumes reading. COBY sits on the floor next to KATHERINE, leans against her, closes her eyes. LUCAS enters the day room, checking out the place. He sees COBY and KATHERINE, then sees JOEL. He watches him for a moment in disbelief.)

LUCAS. Joel.

DYING GIRL *(relieved to see him)*. Lucas.

JOEL. You got in.

LUCAS. Yeah, I told them I was Katherine Lewis' cousin. Where is she?

JOEL. There.

LUCAS. Hi. Hi, Katherine, I'm a friend of Joel's…

JOEL. She won't talk to you.

LUCAS. She…she doesn't move?

JOEL. Not now.

LUCAS *(turning to JOEL. After a moment)*. What are they doing to you?

JOEL. Locking me in…giving me drugs.

DEMON *(with disdain)*. Drugs…

DYING GIRL *(with hope)*. Lucas…

JOEL. Will you…can you stay here awhile?

LUCAS. Sure. *(As LUCAS sits next to JOEL, the DEMON literally moves farther away from JOEL.)*

DYING GIRL *(to DEMON, delighted)*. Where are you going? *(DEMON hisses at her.)*

LUCAS *(indicating JULIE)*. Who is that?

JOEL. Julie.

LUCAS. What's going on?

JOEL. I don't know.

JULIE. We're leaving soon.

LUCAS *(again looks around room, takes in the others)*. Did you want to tell me something?

JOEL. Yeah. Tell Beth I'm sorry.

LUCAS. All right. *(Silence.)*

JOEL. Do you think...I should be here?

LUCAS. I don't know.

HOLLY *(sings louder. See the following page for what occurs while she's singing this part of the song)*.

    AND YES, THAT WATER,
    COOL AND CLEAR,
    SINGS ETERNAL FOR ALL TO HEAR.
    SINGS A LIVING MYSTERY.
    OVER EVERY LAKE AND EVERY SEA.
    AND YES, THAT WATER,
    COOL AND CLEAR,
    SINGS ETERNAL FOR ALL TO HEAR

    AND NO CREATURE ON THE WATER
    LAND OR SKY,
    NO WOMAN, MAN OR CHILD SHALL EVER CRY,
    ON THIS SPHERE,
    WITHOUT THE WATER CATCHING EVERY
      TEAR.

**WITHOUT THE WATER CATCHING EVERY
TEAR.
WITHOUT THE WATER CATCHING EVERY
TEAR."**

DURING SONG:

*(RICK gets up, gets a bag of muffins, moves back close
to HOLLY, begins eating muffins. Then:*

*BETH gets up, moves away from the others, looks out
over the water. Then:*

*JOEL, with JULIE sitting up against him and LUCAS
sitting next to him, begins rocking back and forth.
JULIE rocks with him. Then:*

*TOM moves to COBY, sits down next to her, leans
against her as she is leaning against KATHERINE.
Then:*

*TRISHA enters beach, walks over to BETH, they em-
brace. Then:*

*JOEL's look around room, at JULIE, KATHERINE,
COBY; the hospital, the locked door; LUCAS.)*

HOLLY FINISHES SONG.

JOEL *(stops rocking)*. I can't believe this. *(Fade-out.)*

END ACT I

ACT II

SCENE I

SCENE: *Day room, afternoon, three days later.*

AT RISE: *TOM ushers in BETH and LUCAS. During this scene, BETH becomes increasingly anxious about her surroundings.*

LUCAS. How long will his session last?

TOM. Only a few more minutes. The doctor is usually quite prompt.

BETH. How is he doing? I mean, do they know what's wrong with him?

TOM. If they knew they wouldn't tell me.

BETH. Don't you work here?

TOM. Oh, no. I'm a patient.

BETH. Oh.

TOM. Can't you tell?

BETH. I couldn't.

LUCAS. I couldn't.

TOM. That's great, because I get out on Friday. When I first came, I—and you may laugh at this—I thought I was Jesus Christ. Isn't that crazy?

BETH. Probably.

LUCAS. Probably.

TOM. Me, Jesus. Ha. You should have seen me last Good Friday. *(He holds out his arms, sings an angelic note, laughs.)* That...was not a good day. Therapy here has taught me a lot about myself. Obviously I'm the Antichrist. *(LUCAS and BETH don't know what to say to this.)* I'll let Joel's nurse know he has visitors waiting. *(He exits.)*

BETH. Well, that was weird.

LUCAS. Yeah.

BETH. Was he serious?

LUCAS. I couldn't tell.

(JULIE walks in holding a series of feathers. She sees BETH, stares at her, clearly fearful.)

LUCAS. Hi.

JULIE *(slowly walks around them, looking directly at BETH the whole time. Quietly, in fear)*. Beth... *(She exits.)*

BETH. Did she say my name?

LUCAS. Yes she did.

BETH. How did she know my name?

(COBY comes in leading KATHERINE. KATHERINE is still catatonic but lets COBY lead her slowly, stiffly, into room, toward her chair. COBY senses an opportunity here.)

COBY. You must be Lucas and Beth. Oh, I always get this part confused. Which is which? Don't tell me! What do you think, Katherine? *(Whenever COBY moves KATHERINE, KATHERINE allows it, but she moves slowly and stiffly—not in jerks, but with constant resistance. COBY puts KATHERINE's arm out, fixes KATHERINE's hand so it looks like she's pointing at BETH. COBY puts KATHERINE's other hand on KATHERINE's hip. COBY takes her hands away and KATHERINE's arms and hands stay where COBY has put them. KATHERINE's arms remain there through the following. Standing be-hind KATHERINE, as a very bad ventriloquist; to BETH and LUCAS.)* You can both go to hell in a Volkswagen. *(As herself, to KATHERINE.)* Oh, you nut. Be nice, Princess. *(As herself, to BETH and LUCAS.)* Don't mind her. She swears at everybody. *(As KATHERINE.)* She looks like a cheap streetwalker. Somebody should tell her. *(As herself, to KATHERINE.)* She'll find out herself. And if you can't say something nice don't say anything at all. *(As KATHERINE, to BETH.)* You look like a tart, sister. Who did your make-up—your gerbil? *(As herself, slapping KATHERINE's hand.)* That's not nice. She probably doesn't even have a gerbil. Be kind; it's her first time. *(As KATHERINE.)* What does she want? Oh, I recognize her. *(To BETH.)* You'll have to get your drugs elsewhere, honey. We're clean. *(As herself, to KATHER-INE.)* They don't want drugs...tonight. They're here to visit Joel. *(As KATHERINE.)* Oh, the screamer, the drummer. Keeps everybody up all night. Crazy bastard. Tell him to take his meds. *(As she begins to lead KATH-ERINE to her chair.)* You're funny, Katherine. You say the craziest things. *(As KATHERINE, as she puts her in chair.)* Look at them two. Looks like they're standing on top of a wedding cake. Somebody should drop a Buick on them. *(KATHERINE is seated. COBY moves to*

LUCAS. In a soft, sexy voice.) Hello. My name is Coby. Coby, do you know what that's short for?

LUCAS. No.

COBY *(continuing in a soft, sexy voice).* You're kind of dumb, ain't you. That's sweet. Coby, that's short for Cobra. You know what a Cobra is?

LUCAS. Yeah.

COBY. Oh, I'm excited. What is a cobra?

LUCAS. A car.

COBY. Oh, darlin', you are dumb. That is so sexy in a man. A cobra is a snake. You want to see my tattoo?

LUCAS. Sure. *(She begins to undo her belt. LUCAS and BETH look for help.)*

BETH. Oh, no.

LUCAS. I don't think I want to see that.

COBY. You won't believe your eyes.

LUCAS. I haven't believed anything since I got here.

COBY. It makes a snaky noise; it says: Sssssssucker. *(She bursts out laughing, then does a series of quick takes exaggerating BETH's and LUCAS' responses to her. As BETH and LUCAS:)* "Oh. Oh, no! What do I do? I don't think I want to see that!" *(She laughs.)* Hey! It's been fun messing with your minds, but I got to go to the can. *(She hurries off.)*

BETH. And it's going to help him being in here? This place would make me crazy.

(JOEL enters, looking drugged.)

BETH. Joel!

JOEL. Beth! You came!

BETH. Of course I came. That's all right, isn't it? *(They embrace. He holds on tight.)*

JOEL. Oh, you came. You're here. Thank you.

BETH. Of course I'm here. *(She begins to pull away, he pulls her back, hugs her tightly. From a deeper source:)* Of course I'm here.

JOEL. Beth...

LUCAS. Hi, Joel. I'm here too.

JOEL. Lucas. *(He gradually releases her, but holds her hand.)*

BETH. How are you? You look tired, but, you look better—are you doing better?

JOEL. Yeah, but they got me locked in here with all these weird people.

BETH. I know! I've met some of them!

JOEL. A couple remind me of you, Lucas. Especially this chick named Coby.

LUCAS. Yeah, I see the resemblance.

JOEL. Have you met Katherine?

LUCAS. Yeah.

JOEL. She's tough, but I beat her in arm-wrestling. *(He puts her arm up, struggles, then pushes it down. Impulsively, BETH embraces him again, holds onto him tightly.)* Just because I beat her in arm-wrestling, doesn't mean I like her more than you.

BETH. I'm just scared, that's all.

JOEL. I'm not going to hurt you.

BETH. I'm scared for you. And I'm scared of myself. Of what I might do.

JOEL. What do your parents want you to do? *(She releases him, then moves away. Anxiously.)* Where are you going?

BETH. I brought your drumsticks. *(She hands him his sticks, and cookies.)* And some cookies.

JOEL. Thanks. *(He takes her hand again.)*

BETH. They think I shouldn't see you for a while. Until you're feeling better and you understand what happened. They're afraid you might do something to me.

(He lets her hand go, she takes his back. TOM enters with JULIE, who is carrying her feathers. She starts toward JOEL.)

TOM. Julie, you know what the doctor said. *(JULIE stops, looks at JOEL in fear.)*

JOEL. Hi, Julie.

JULIE. My therapist says I shouldn't hug you without asking your permission. May I hug you now?

JOEL. Julie, this is Beth. Beth, this is my new friend Julie.

BETH. Hello, Julie.

JULIE. I saw them before. And then they came, today, to get you but, they don't know, yet, that they can't take you. They don't know who you are. I do. May I hug you now?

JOEL. What's my name?

JULIE. Joel. Jacob died.

JOEL. Yes, you may hug me. *(Delighted, she instantly brightens, goes to him, and they embrace. JULIE holds on tightly. BETH registers surprise, but not jealousy.)*

TOM. That was nice, Julie.

JULIE. We have a dream.

COBY *(entering, goosing LUCAS)*. Hey!

LUCAS. Ah!

COBY. It's a Joel party! Where's the pizza and beer?

LUCAS *(rubbing his bottom).* It's not back here.

JOEL *(as JULIE holds on).* Coby, Tom, this is Beth and this is Lucas.

TOM. Hello.

COBY. I got them confused. No wonder I'm in here. Cute couple.

JOEL. Beth is *my* girlfriend.

COBY. Better not let Julie hear you say that. *(Seeing JULIE.)* Where is she anyway?

JULIE. Here.

COBY. Then Lucas, you're a free man?

LUCAS. Ye...yeah.

COBY. I'm getting out this weekend.

LUCAS. That's...great.

COBY. You want to jump on my Harley and watch the sunrise? It'll change your life.

LUCAS. Whoa, baby, no doubt.

COBY *(moves close to LUCAS, touching him. She speaks seductively, but in Spanish.) Yo se que tu madre fue una compasina cuidano cerdos, y tu padre comio' ratas. Naciste en una Casa de coyotes y hueles como una vaca.* (She laughs at him.)*

LUCAS *(suddenly taking her in his arms). Gracias, mi amor, por decir cosas tan bonitas. Soy tuyo para siempre.** (He pushes COBY away, confident of his revenge. COBY laughs, raises her hand.)*

COBY. Hey, it's official: I like you. *(LUCAS and COBY slap hands.)*

---

* I know your mother was a pig farmer and your father ate rats. You were born in a coyote den and you smell like a cow.

** Thank you, my love, for saying those beautiful things to me. I am yours forever.

LUCAS. Hey, that's amazing. I am one lucky El White Guy.

COBY. Hey, what you got? *(Takes box of cookies from JOEL, opens it.)* Cookies! *(She eats one and brings the box to KATHERINE.)* Look, Katherine, someone gave us cookies! *(She puts one in KATHERINE's mouth. After COBY has taken a bite of one herself, she'll help KATHERINE rise and they'll both exit.)*

JULIE. We have a dream. We're going to live inside tall, faraway walls that no one can climb. We're going to build a house, with a porch, and with peacocks. I have their feathers, see?

BETH. Yes, I see.

JULIE. We're going to get out together. It's why he's here; this time he's going to take me with him. So you can't go to college with Lucas and Beth.

JOEL. Thank you, Julie. You may let go of me now.

JULIE. But I have to talk to you.

JOEL. Let me go.

JULIE. But I haven't told you about our dream.

JOEL. I feel like you're strangling me. Let me go.

JULIE. Jacob!

JOEL. I'm not Jacob! I'm Joel!

TOM. Julie, be nice.

JULIE *(unwraps from him. Frightened, reassuring herself)*. I'll be here when they go home, like last night.

TOM. Are you all right, Julie? *(JULIE exits. TOM follows her out.)*

BETH. What was that about?

JOEL. That was Julie.

BETH. Wow.

JOEL *(taking her hand again)*. I like *our* dream.

BETH *(sings to JOEL).* " 'Cause I won't give up on my dreams."

JOEL *(brighter).* You're singing to me.

BETH *(sings, as JOEL looks deeply into her).* "No I won't give up on my dreams."

LUCAS. She had Holly teach her.

BETH *(sings).* "You say you're out of your mind."

JOEL *(joking).* No kidding!

BETH *(sings, from "Dreams").*

> **TO LEAVE IT ALL BEHIND.**
> **BUT I WON'T GIVE UP ON MY DREAMS.**
> **OOO, OOO, OOO.**
> **WON'T GIVE UP ON MY DREAMS.**
> **OOO, OOO, OOO.** *(She kisses him.)*

JOEL. Thank you.

BETH. Anytime you want I'll sing. I've been learning a couple of songs just for you.

JOEL. Thanks; I'm going to be fine, now, with you singing!

BETH. Anytime. I'm not giving up.

JOEL. Did you call about summer orientation?

BETH. Yeah.

JOEL. You did?

BETH. I'm going the same week as you guys.

JOEL. Yes! We are gone! We'll leave it all behind! We'll be there together! I made some calls today about an apartment for next year—an on-campus apartment. They're not as expensive as I thought. It's looking good, Lucas.

LUCAS *(without a strong commitment).* Yeah.

JOEL. But you have to call about summer orientation. You haven't set your date, yet, for summer orientation. You have to call them because they wouldn't let me sign you up and we have to go together.

LUCAS. All right.

JOEL. How long can you stay?

BETH. A couple hours.

JOEL *(relieved)*. Great. A couple hours. You look good, to-day. Doesn't she? You look good. *Beth*…"all that's best of dark and bright…" *(Short silence.)*

BETH. Joel, what's going on with you?

JOEL. Ah, I talk enough about that in here. *(He drops her hand. To LUCAS.)* What's the news with Laura? Is she going to orientation week with us?

BETH. Joel, please, talk to me; I'm scared to death.

JOEL. I hate these drugs. They make my mouth dry, I feel shaky all the time—I feel like a zombie. I don't know what is wrong with me. But I am not mentally ill. I've seen people who are mentally ill, and I'm not. *(To LUCAS.)* Have you seen her? Is she coming to our next game?

LUCAS. I think you should tell her, Joel. And maybe I'll learn something new so I can help you.

JOEL *(to BETH)*. Is that why you came today?

BETH. I came to see you.

JOEL *(after a moment)*. You can't tell the doctors or any of the hospital staff.

LUCAS. I won't.

BETH. You know I won't.

JOEL. Promise me, Lucas.

LUCAS. I promise.

JOEL. You still owe me for that Chicago trip.

LUCAS. And I ate half the chocolates Beth gave you for your birthday.

BETH. I thought that was your mom!
JOEL. So did I.
LUCAS. So, yes, I mean it.

(ROCK AND ROLL DRUMS FADE IN QUIETLY. These
are drums of a single person on a complete drum set,
playing by himself, as JOEL would. The beat is strong,
but never wild or frenetic. It follows JOEL's speech
rhythms and contains variations and flourishes. It is as
much music as percussion. Lights dim and isolate JOEL,
BETH and LUCAS.)

JOEL. I hear drums most of the time in here…it helps me
    (JOEL uses drums to hold VOICES at a distance. He
    does this by putting the drums into his body and his
    mind, and moving to the beat. He begins this now.) I
    wanted to tell you what I've been thinking, anyway. And
    I'll tell you about some of them.
BETH. Some of who?
JOEL. Some of the ones…who talk to me.

(DEMON enters. LUCAS and BETH do not watch the
VOICES directly. They watch JOEL, as if he is telling
them what the VOICES are saying.)

LUCAS. Do you ask them to talk to you?
JOEL. They talk whenever they want.
LUCAS. Can you stop them?
JOEL. Of course not. He…he was first. And for a while, he
    helped me, he tries to protect me, but—
DEMON. Do what I tell you, or they will die, I'll burn
    them in a fire like the others; listen to me. Go to your

room, open your arm, and write in your blood the names of those you killed. *(He moves upstage and stands staring at JOEL. Again, BETH and LUCAS do not react directly to VOICES but to JOEL, as if JOEL has just told them what the DEMON said.)*

BETH. God, Joel.

LUCAS. Oh, so now it's more than one guy you killed?

JOEL *(as the GHOST enters)*. He, ah, I told you about him. I killed him, and he won't leave, he won't stop, and he wants—

GHOST. Coward, afraid to die, you need to die, take your poison. Go to your room and take your poison. Die in your sleep and be a blessed ghost. Die, and redeem yourself. *(He slowly slides to the floor, sits, looking up at JOEL.)*

BETH. Why do you hear these things?

JOEL. Yes! That's what I was thinking!

LUCAS. You don't have to listen to them—

JOEL. Ha!

LUCAS. All right, you don't have to do what they say.

JOEL. And she... *(DYING GIRL enters.)* She does help me; she cares for me. She wants what I want—to move away from here and go to college—she likes you, Beth, she wants me to marry you, but sometimes—

DYING GIRL. How could you hurt me like this? Don't let me die. You loved me once. Give me my future. Our future. We have so much to do together. Leave this place and figure out how to heal me. I'll stay with you a long time. *(The VOICES form a large, rough triangle around JOEL. QUIET DRUMS FADE OUT. Agitated, JOEL paces between the VOICES, pushing through the drugs, desperately looking for answers.)*

JOEL *(to BETH; rhythmic, pressured, rapid speech)*. But you said it. Exactly what I keep thinking— Why?— Why did this happen to me and not you or Lucas or Rick, there must be a reason. *(DYING GIRL sits.)* I have to ask Trisha why it happened to her—but I'm not like her, my head swells, I'm allergic to something—or maybe it *is* I'm being punished.

LUCAS. You-haven't-killed-any-body.

JOEL. How would you know?— You don't know.

LUCAS. How do you know?

JOEL *(referring to GHOST)*. Because he tells me.

LUCAS. I told you: I can't hear him. He's not there.

JOEL. I know he's telling the truth. It doesn't make sense any other way.

LUCAS. Where's the body?

JOEL. You'll never find it.

BETH. Because there isn't one.

JOEL. Because it rotted away.

LUCAS. Then how can he talk to you?

JOEL. Because I killed him.

LUCAS. But how can he talk to you if his mouth has rotted away?

JOEL. Because I killed him.

LUCAS *(changing the direction)*. Did you ask the doctor why he looks like you?

JOEL. What does the doctor know?

LUCAS. What did he say?

JOEL *(as his psychiatrist)*. "Do you think it might be you? Or a part of you?"

LUCAS. It is, isn't it?

JOEL. Ha!

LUCAS. He's you. It's not somebody else. He's dressed like you, he talks like you. It's *you!* You're making this up. It's in your head.

JOEL *(dismissing this, shaking his head)*. It's why Coleridge wrote that poem about me.

BETH. He wrote *Ancient Mariner* about you?

JOEL. Of course—of course.

LUCAS. What year did he write it?

JOEL. 1798.

LUCAS. What year did he die?

JOEL. 1834.

LUCAS. Then how could he have known you and written a poem about you?

JOEL *(looking in the GHOST's eyes)*.

"An orphan's curse would drag to hell,

A spirit from on high;

But oh! more horrible than that

Is the curse in a dead man's eye!"

You see? It's all about me. And the answer is in there, somewhere. You see?— It's in there.

BETH. No, Joel, that doesn't make any sense.

LUCAS. OK, then how, in the poem, did he get the albatross to drop off his neck?

JOEL *(to DYING GIRL)*.

"A spring of love gushed from my heart,

And I blessed them unaware…"

LUCAS. And that's what you have to do? see something so beautiful a spring of love gushes from your heart?

JOEL *(taking DYING GIRL's hand, looking into her eyes)*. That's why he wrote it about me; to tell me what I had to do— I have to do something like that.

LUCAS. So why don't you do it?!

JOEL *(breaks from DYING GIRL, resumes pacing).* I tried— With you— *(BETH.)* —on the beach— And out in the boat— I thought I did. I thought maybe last Saturday at your house. I thought today when I first saw you—I was so glad to see you—and again later I felt it when I looked at you—didn't you?—and then you sang! I thought, now, right now, I love her right now! But, but I have to do it when I'm unaware and it just hasn't happened yet, not yet, I haven't done it, yet— I'll never do it on these damn drugs! But when I do, we'll be set for college. I'm going to get that apartment, we'll live in an apartment and it'll be great, it'll be perfect for us, we'll all be at school and safe and together. That's our dream. That's my dream. That's what's going to happen.

LUCAS. I may not be able to go.

BETH. What?

JOEL. Why not?— What did you say?— You may not go?— Is that what you said?— Why?— Money? Is that it, money?

LUCAS. I shouldn't have said anything.

JOEL. I'm not going without you—I can't go without you. Jesus! I can't go without you!

BETH. He'll go; he'll find a way.

LUCAS. I'll find a way. I'll go.

JOEL. That's right.

LUCAS. I will.

JOEL. OK.

LUCAS. I'll go with you.

JOEL. I need to understand it, Lucas—and I will, I will, but I can't think, it's hard to think, how can I think with all these sick people around me!—and these drugs—

they're trying to control me with these drugs—and I can't—

LUCAS. You're tired. You need to stop. You need to stop thinking. You need to sleep. They told me to tell you to sleep.

JOEL. I need to know why.

LUCAS *(finally gives up. In a helpless sadness)*. I don't know what to do. God, Joel, I don't know what to do.

JOEL. Help me figure it out.

LUCAS. I don't know what to say to you. I can't believe this.

JOEL. I know.

LUCAS. You're scaring the hell out of me, Joel. What's going to happen to you?

JOEL. I'll get it— I'll figure it out— I'm figuring it out.

LUCAS. What can I do?

JOEL. Tell me the truth.

LUCAS. I am, but it doesn't seem to help.

JOEL. Yeah it does.

LUCAS. What can I do? *(LUCAS sits in helplessness.)*

JOEL. Maybe he knows. He was first. *(i.e., the DEMON. It moves toward JOEL.)* He used to help me. Maybe he knows what I have to do. *(DRUMS COME IN AT MODERATE VOLUME. JOEL begins putting the drumbeat into his body and mind to hold the VOICES back. Again, the drums never get frenetic; although they get louder and more intense, they're always under control. The drums fit the scene, they're not paced too fast; they feed off the rhythm of the scene, and JOEL in turn plays off the drums.)*

    The many men, so beautiful,
    And they all dead did lie;

And a thousand thousand slimy things
Lived on and so did I.

(DRUMS CONTINUE PLAYING under the following:)

JOEL *(cont'd)*. What do I have to do?

DEMON. I've seen you. I know where you've been, I've seen the pain and the death, you have done hellish things; you cannot be cleansed of your crimes; you told them you killed one man, but it was more. I was there, I helped you, I know who you are, Miller the Killer.

BETH. This isn't true, Joel.

JOEL *(to BETH)*. Listen! You wanted to know what was going on. This is what's going on! *(To DYING GIRL.)* What do I have to do?

DYING GIRL *(moving into him. JOEL looks each of the VOICES in the face when they speak to him. He continues to move to the drums, successfully holding VOICES off)*. How could you hurt me like this? Don't you care? Don't let me die. You loved me once. Give me my future. Our future. We have so much to do together.

JOEL. How? What do I have to do?

BETH. Who is she? Where does she come from?

GHOST. I'll tell you what to do.

JOEL *(GHOST rises, moves to JOEL)*.

I looked upon the rotting sea,
And drew my eyes away;
I looked upon the rotting deck,
And there the dead men lay.

GHOST *(indicating himself and DYING GIRL)*. See the truth. See who you are. This is what you do. You are not one of them, anymore. *(Indicates LUCAS and BETH.)* They are good; they're healthy, like you used to be.

You're dead, now, like me. When you killed me, you killed yourself.

BETH. You didn't kill anybody! *(Louder DRUMS. Each VOICE pursues JOEL when it speaks. He continues moving to drums, still holding them at an emotional distance.)*

DYING GIRL. You did this to me. You can stop it. Help me. We'll go away; our plans, remember our plans.

DEMON. You deserve the pain, you deserve the fear, you deserve the hate. You do not deserve them. *(Re BETH and LUCAS.)*

BETH. This isn't true, Joel. None of this is true.

DEMON. Send them away. Or I will. Send them away! Or they'll fall in pieces down a hole.

DYING GIRL. You did this to me. You can heal me. Leave this place and figure out how to heal me. Take me with you. I'll go with you. I'll stay with you a long time. You're the only one who can heal me.

DEMON. Let her die. Take Julie with you. Julie knows you; listen to her. She'll help you. You belong with her.

GHOST. Tell them who you are, you killed us, killed us all, tell them your name: Miller the Killer, Miller the Killer. A thousand slimy things live on, and so do you.

(DRUMS COME UP, now, stronger and louder. JOEL tries to move from the DEMON and GHOST, but they head him off. The VOICES now begin to penetrate him.)

(The next two speech are delivered simultaneously.)

DEMON. Listen to me, do what I say or I will go after them, the ones who love you; do what I tell you, or they will die, I'll burn them in a fire; listen to me. Go to your room, open your arm, and write in your blood the names of those you killed.

GHOST. Coward, afraid to die, coward, you need to die, take your poison. Go to your room and take your poison. Die in your sleep and be a blessed ghost. A blessed ghost. Die, and redeem yourself.

(Louder, stronger DRUMS. The VOICES are breaking into JOEL and he is clearly suffering, frantically trying to hold them off by focusing on and moving to the drums. VOICES circle JOEL.)

(The next three speeches are delivered simultaneously.)

DEMON. Go now, or your friends will die in the fire. Listen to me, in your blood, on the walls, write the names of those you killed, Miller the Killer, Miller the Killer, Miller the Killer. Bleed. Bleed.

DYING GIRL. How could you hurt me like this? Don't let me die. You loved me once. Give me my future. Our future. We have so much to do together. Leave this place and figure out how to heal me. I'll go with you. I'll stay with you a long time. You're the only one who can heal me. Joel. Joel!

GHOST. Coward, afraid to die, coward, you need to die, take your poison. Go to your room and open your arm. Die in your sleep and become a blessed ghost. A blessed ghost. Die, and redeem yourself.

(The above three speeches repeat and begin repeating again.)

(DRUMS become louder and more intense. JOEL rocks in place as the VOICES circle him. This rocking is both

rocking back and forth and almost dancing. He now stares at the floor about ten feet in front of him, trying to drown out the VOICES, but they are breaking into him. He holds his head and writhes as he's rocking. The DRUMS SUDDENLY END in the middle of an intense section, JOEL screams, grabs his head, falls to his knees. He continues screaming in pain, as the DEMON, DYING GIRL and GHOST recede, and are much quieter, but continue repeating their lines together.)

BETH. Joel… *(She tries to hold JOEL but he pushes her away.)* Joel, it's Beth.

(She tries again, again he pushes her away. He stops screaming, groans, trying to push the VOICES out of his head with his hands. JULIE runs on to JOEL, embraces him. JOEL lets her hold him. The VOICES exit still speaking.)

JULIE. We'll go away. Then, after we die, when we live inside our high walls, we won't hurt anymore. *(JOEL suddenly fully embraces her. LUCAS watches their embrace for a moment, then rips JULIE away from JOEL, pushes her away.)* Don't touch me! Let me go! Let me go! Joel!
LUCAS. Stay away from him! *(He goes to JOEL, who has his head in his hands. LUCAS wants to say or do something, but doesn't know what to do. JOEL looks up at him. LUCAS pulls him up. Finally, impulsively, LUCAS hugs him. Tableau. Blackout.)*

SCENE II

SCENE: *Dusk, four weeks later, on Joel's beach. As in first scene, the table is set for a gathering: chairs, food, coolers.*

AT RISE: *TRISHA enters carrying a bag of drinks. She sees no one is there, sets bag down.*

TRISHA *(this time she is not especially anxious).* Spying on me again?... No, I wasn't spying on you; I wanted to make sure you got here on time... You got me here so early I'm the first one here, again... Who are you going to be, tonight, you, or me?... I don't have to be you with these people.

(Again, TRISHA dances on the shore to amuse herself. RICK and HOLLY enter. TRISHA continues to dance absently. HOLLY carries her guitar, RICK a big bag of munchies.)

RICK/HOLLY/TRISHA. Trisha!/Hey, girl./Hi.
RICK. Where is everybody?
TRISHA. You're a little early.
RICK *(dumping his bag on the table).* Because I'd hate to have to eat all this myself.
HOLLY. Beautiful night for a party.
RICK. Any bodies buried out here tonight?
TRISHA. I haven't seen any, but the party is just starting.
HOLLY. Was someone here? Who were you talking to?
TRISHA *(laughs nervously, stops dancing).* I was talking to myself.

HOLLY *(getting her guitar out. To TRISHA)*. How's Joel
    doing? Must be doing well if they're letting him out af-
    ter only a couple of weeks.

TRISHA. I saw him two days ago in the hospital and he
    was doing better. They give you medication, patch you
    up, get you out the door as soon as possible, and send
    you to a therapist.

HOLLY. Is he still saying those things?

TRISHA. Not as much. But that might be just because he
    knows how other people react to it. You kind of learn
    that? To keep a lot of what's going on in your head to
    yourself. Otherwise, people look at you like you're from
    Mars and you're alone too much.

RICK. What am I supposed to say to the psycho-ward peo-
    ple?

TRISHA. What do you say to me?

RICK. I say: Hey, Trisha. I love the way you dance.

TRISHA. That's fine. Just say whatever you want.

HOLLY. Is there anything we should know to do?

TRISHA. If things get tense, just sing, Holly. That'll make
    everyone calm down.

RICK. Let me know if you need my help for anything.
    (RICK moves off, sits by himself.)

HOLLY. How many are coming?

TRISHA. I don't know. We'll see. I hope Coby comes. I
    want you to meet her; she's great.

HOLLY. Rick.

RICK. What?

HOLLY. What's the matter?

RICK. Nothing.

HOLLY. Why aren't you eating?

RICK. I'm thinking.

HOLLY. You'll fall asleep. You'll miss Joel's party. *(Softer.)* It'll be all right. Joel's feeling much better.

RICK. I'm thinking about you.

HOLLY. I told you not to do that. You get that look in your eye and then you look at me and I feel like I'm a bucket of cheese balls.

RICK *(looking at her, dreamily).* Yeah... *(Back to being firm.)* I'm not saying anything until I have more witnesses.

HOLLY. You're not going to ask me to wear your jersey to the prom again, are you?

RICK. I told you. I'm not talking until I have more witnesses here. But that *is* a great idea.

(JOEL and LUCAS enter. LUCAS carries as many beach chairs as is humanly possible. JOEL carries two small wrapped boxes. He seems calmer and more awake.)

LUCAS. Talk to me.

JOEL. I'm not telling you.

LUCAS. What's inside?

JOEL. You don't tell people what's inside their gifts before they open them.

LUCAS. Well I didn't give *you* a coming-home present.

JOEL. I didn't expect you to.

LUCAS. I didn't know we were giving coming-home presents. Nobody told me we were giving coming-home presents. I didn't buy anybody a single coming-home present.

JOEL. It's all right, man.

LUCAS. Trisha. And Holly and Rick. Look, Joel, it's Trisha, Holly and Rick. You invited three women to the same party again! *(RICK lunges toward LUCAS who flinches, they smile at each other.)*

ALL. Hey, hi, etc.

LUCAS. And why do I always have to carry all the chairs? *(He drops them.)* I told you: It's his beach. *(LUCAS sets up chairs around beach.)*

JOEL *(hands him the box)*. Don't open it until later. *(To TRISHA.)* Have you seen Tom?

TRISHA. Not yet.

JOEL. Is Coby coming?

TRISHA. She promised she would.

(BETH enters with DYING GIRL.)

DYING GIRL. Joel… *(BETH proceeds into crowd toward JOEL, DYING GIRL follows.)*

BETH. Hi, Joel!

LUCAS. Beth. Look, Joel, it's Beth. Without Laura.

BETH. Hey, everybody. *(She embraces JOEL. DYING GIRL puts her hands and head on JOEL's back, leans in to him during embrace.)* Welcome back!

DYING GIRL *(this is a good thing)*. Beth is here.

BETH. Congratulations! *(She hands him a rose and a wrapped gift.)* Open it when you're alone. *(Ooos from the group.)*

LUCAS. Nobody told me we were giving coming-home presents.

JOEL. Good to see you. *(He kisses her, gives her the box he brought.)* Here.

LUCAS. That's another coming-home present.

JOEL. Open it when you're alone with me. *(More ooos from the crowd.)*

LUCAS. Laura parking the car?

BETH. She said she had a party with Randy.

LUCAS. Did she send a note for me?

BETH. I'm sorry, Lucas.

LUCAS. Did she tell you to say anything to me? *(She indicates no.)* Ah. Well, I guess I don't have to paint their house.

(COBY enters.)

COBY. What's shakin'?

JOEL/TRISHA/COBY. Hey, look who came./ Coby!/Artiste!

(COBY and TRISHA embrace.)

LUCAS. Coby. Look, Joel, it's Coby.

JOEL *(embracing COBY)*. Coby, I'm glad you're here. Everybody, this is Coby!

COBY. And look who I brought along.

(COBY goes offstage, returns leading a catatonic KATH-ERINE. The others go quiet. KATHERINE wears a stylish, expensive outfit and a party hat and carries a noise-maker.)

LUCAS. Katherine. Look, Joel, it's Katherine.

TRISHA. She's not moving, again.

JOEL. What happened?

TRISHA. How did you get her out?

RICK. Whoa! What is her deal?

HOLLY. Rick!

RICK. What? Trisha told me I can say anything I want.

HOLLY. She doesn't know you. *(Beat.)* Does she.

RICK. No.

HOLLY. All right.

COBY *(leading her)*. Come on, Katherine, you know almost everyone here. It's a party. You're the Princess of Parties. Maybe later we can go for a boat ride.

KATHERINE *(suddenly bursts into life, startling everyone but COBY)*. Hey, it's a party! *(She blows a noisemaker.)* Party! Party! Beach party! *(She blows noisemaker. Silence. She rips off her party hat and throws it at COBY.)* I told you it wouldn't be funny, you stupid cow! No one's laughing! *(They all burst out laughing.)* I don't know why I came here, anyway. I don't even know half these people. I hate riding in boats. And this beach is full of...*sand!*

RICK. Can I say something, now?

LUCAS, JOEL, TRISHA, BETH & COBY. NO!

HOLLY. Yes.

RICK. What is her deal? *(KATHERINE walks slowly up to RICK. The others watch with interest. RICK is now more anxious.)*

KATHERINE. Who are you?

RICK. Hey.

KATHERINE. What?

RICK. I said hey.

KATHERINE. What the hell does that mean? "Hey." Is that your name—Hey?

RICK. It means: "Hello."

KATHERINE. Hello.

RICK. Hey.

KATHERINE. Who are you?

HOLLY. Talk to her.

RICK. I'm a Taurus. I have a seventh house transit going on. And my Venus is suffering, man.

KATHERINE. What the hell are you talking about?

RICK. I don't know. I'm with her. We talk to dead people.

KATHERINE. What?

RICK. That's kind of crazy, isn't it?

KATHERINE. Do you have a name, Hey?

RICK. Fatboy. Truckbutt.

HOLLY. Rick!

RICK. What?

HOLLY. Talk nice to her!

RICK *(holding out his hand to KATHERINE)*. Excuse me, my name is Rick. I'm pleased to meet you.

KATHERINE. Somebody shoot this son of a bitch and put him out of my misery.

HOLLY. You see, Rick? You'll have no trouble getting dates in college.

KATHERINE *(walks up to JOEL, face to face)*. And don't think I'll ever forget you arm-wrestling with me when I was sick, screamy boy. You want to try it now?

JOEL. Take your meds, today?

KATHERINE. That's none of your damn business.

JOEL. I hope I did. Or I'm going to have an anxiety attack with you this close. *(He smiles.)*

COBY. Katherine, remember, it's a party. *(To crowd.)* And guess what? We're going to take the GED this summer.

KATHERINE. They should just give me the damn diploma. I put up with their crap for enough years.

COBY. And we're quitting smoking, together. *(The others cheer.)*

KATHERINE. Over your dead body.

RICK. Hey, I got something to say.

KATHERINE. More?!

RICK. To Holly! I got something to say to Holly. I need you guys to be my witnesses. *(They quiet down.)* I been reading that stuff you gave me about charts and the planets and it says there's always a *Free-Will Factor*— it's up to the person to decide what's really going to happen.

JOEL *(chanting)*. Free will. *(Others join in.)*

GROUP. Free will! Free will!

RICK. That's true, isn't it? Isn't it?

HOLLY. Well, yes.

RICK. We can *decide* to stay together no matter what those charts say.

(The next five speeches are said simultaneously.)

BETH. Rick, I'm impressed.

TRISHA. Right. That's right.

JOEL. Yeah, free will. Free will!

COBY. That's the way it is, baby.

LUCAS. All right Rick, you tell her.

KATHERINE *(starting before they have all finished)*. What a load of crap!

RICK. So don't be kissing me off just yet.

HOLLY. I won't kiss you off if you stop trying to make long-term plans. You have to allow for things we never even dreamed of coming our way.

RICK. Nothing coming is going to mean more than you. *(The group groans.)*

HOLLY. Ah, Rocko, in front of everybody you said that.

RICK. That's right.

KATHERINE *(groans. Then)*. Ugh. I'm in a group therapy nightmare. Take me back to the hospital.

COBY. Not for a couple hours, so find a reason to have fun.

KATHERINE. Somebody get me a drink.

JOEL. I will. *(JOEL, followed by DYING GIRL, heads for the drinks.)*

DEMON *(entering, cutting him off)*. What a nice party. Am I invited? *(DYING GIRL moves between DEMON and JOEL; JOEL moves to get a drink for KATHERINE; DEMON pushes DYING GIRL aside and shadows JOEL as he brings a drink to KATHERINE. DYING GIRL moves to BETH, stands near her.)*

TRISHA. I see Ronnie's back in town.

COBY. Yeah.

TRISHA. What are you going to do?

COBY. After I graduate I thought I'd go to flight school to become a stewardess.

TRISHA. Oh, that's nice.

COBY. Or maybe go to cosmetology school to learn hair. *(Short silence.)*

TRISHA *(suddenly grinning)*. You're lying! *(KATHERINE, TRISHA and COBY all laugh.)*

COBY. I'm going out West and fight wilderness fires. Thought I'd do some good.

TRISHA. Now that sounds like you. And Ronnie?

COBY. Ronnie's gone.

(Focus shifts.)

BETH *(talking to JOEL)*. Does Lucas know?

GHOST *(entering near JOEL)*. They all know.

LUCAS. What?

GHOST. About me.

BETH. He says he may not go to school with us this fall.

LUCAS. What? Joel… *(Hauls him away from group so the others can't hear them. The VOICES gather around JOEL.)*

DYING GIRL. Remember our future.

LUCAS. Did those voices tell you to do this?

JOEL. I have to stay here for a while and figure this out.

LUCAS. Because I told you, they have to talk to me before they make you do anything.

JOEL. I know what I'm doing, here. I know where I am. I worked out this plan with my doctor. I can do the exercises, eat regular meals, I can sleep here, they can do their "reality orientation therapy" with me—

LUCAS. You can do that stuff at school. Beth can help you.

JOEL. But I have to reduce the dosage of these drugs— that's what Trisha said—to find where I can think and still keep them off me. I have to fight to think. I shouldn't have to fight to think.

LUCAS. You'd be better at school, you love school, you're a great student.

JOEL. My goal is to go, if I can.

DEMON. They'll go without you.

GHOST. You'll never leave this beach.

DEMON. They're different than you.

GHOST. You'll die like me, buried in the sand. *(Reaching out, grabbing JOEL by the throat with one hand. JOEL tries to appear to LUCAS as if nothing is happening, and he is in complete control. JOEL tries unsuccessfully to calmly take the hand from his throat.)*

LUCAS. Joel, we got a lot of time, we got all summer.

DYING GIRL. You have to take us in the fall.

LUCAS. You can't decide that now.

JOEL *(through the hand on his throat)*. Don't you think I would rather go to school with you and Beth? Don't you think I'll do everything I can to get there with you?

LUCAS. Yeah. Yeah I do.

JOEL *(as he talks, begins to finally pull the hand from around his throat)*. This isn't what today is about. *(Through the force of his will, the hand is almost off.)* Your present— *(He pulls hand off.)* Today is about your present. *(JOEL moves to the other people on beach. VOICES back off but remain on stage until the end.)*

LUCAS. Joel—

JOEL. Open your present.

LUCAS. Now?

JOEL. Yeah.

LUCAS *(opening his present)*. But we have to talk about this.

JOEL. We will. Open your present. *(LUCAS takes out a piece of paper, reads it.)*

LUCAS. You can't... You can't do this.

JOEL. I already did. That's a receipt.

LUCAS. Joel, I can't take this.

BETH. What is it?

LUCAS. He's paid the lease on an apartment for a year.

JOEL. In your name, in case I have to come later or... something.

LUCAS. Do your parents know about this?

JOEL. It's my money, I earned it. And it's—what did you call it, Rick?

RICK. I did?

JOEL. Free will. I chose to do it.

LUCAS. I won't be able to pay you back.

JOEL. It's not a loan. You'll probably still have to work this summer, but not as much. Then, while you're at school, your baseball scholarship will cover your tuition so you don't have to work at all.

LUCAS. Joel, you worked hard for that money, for *you* to go school. You need that money.

JOEL *(from a much deeper place)*. I want to do this.

(All VOICES take a step toward him, saying their lines simultaneously. JOEL quiets them with his line.)

GHOST. Don't—

DYING GIRL. But—

DEMON. You—

JOEL. *I* want to. You got to go. Right away, not wait a year. You're ready to go to college the way you never were to high school. So you go. And…and if you take the apartment, it'll be something nothing can take away from me.

LUCAS *(after considering a moment)*. I don't know what to do.

COBY. Take the gift and thank him! I hate it when something good happens and we're too screwed up to appreciate it!

(LAURA appears, followed by TOM and JULIE.)

LUCAS. Laura? And Tom? And Julie. Look, Joel, it's Laura, and Tom and Julie. *(ALL greet.)*

LAURA. I found them wandering the beach.

JOEL. Thanks for bringing Julie, Tom.

TOM. I hope you don't mind that I came, too.

JOEL. I invited you because I wanted you to come.

TOM. That was nice of you, Joel.

JOEL. It was nice of you to come, Tom.

JULIE. Hi, Joel.

JOEL. Hi, Julie.

JULIE. Hi, Beth.

BETH. Hello, Julie.

JOEL. Thanks for coming. Everyone, be nice to my friend Julie. Katherine?

KATHERINE. Just keep that little snake away from me.

JOEL. Lucas?

LUCAS. Yeah.

JULIE. I'll sit over here and wait for you to talk to me.

TOM. I'll sit with you, Julie. *(They move off together and sit. HOLLY PLAYS GUITAR underneath the following.)*

LUCAS *(to LAURA)*. So, you came.

LAURA. I can't stay long. Somebody's waiting for me at the other party.

KATHERINE *(to COBY)*. Can I have a cigarette?

COBY. No.

KATHERINE. I wish I'd never met you.

RICK. Holly...if you won't wear my ring at college next year, will you at least put my poster up in your bathroom?

HOLLY. And you think Joel is strange.

TRISHA *(to herself)*. Are you having a good time? Yeah, go back to sleep. I told you I didn't need you.

JOEL. Did you see Lucas' face when I gave him his present? That was...real, wasn't it.

BETH. Yes it was.

JOEL. That was real.

TOM *(to JULIE)*. How do you like your new foster home?

JULIE. I ran away, tonight. I'm going to stay with Joel.

TRISHA *(to COBY)*. What are you going to do without Ronnie to obsess over?

COBY. Have a damn good time.

LUCAS *(to LAURA)*. By the way, I have a little more free time this summer—for concerts, plays, stargazing—

LAURA. My mother would never understand you.

TOM *(to JULIE)*. Does Joel know you want to stay with him?

JULIE. We're going into our dream, now. This time he's not going alone. He's taking me.

RICK *(HOLLY suddenly stops playing guitar)*. What's the matter?

HOLLY *(suddenly hugs him with tears in her eyes)*. I'll miss you, Rick.

RICK. YEAH, BABY! *(He pulls her onto his lap.)*

LAURA *(to LUCAS)*. So, when's the next time you pitch a home game?

LUCAS *(grinning)*. Tuesday. I'll give you my schedule.

BETH *(to JOEL)*. If you don't go to State in the fall, I'm not either. I can stay here and take classes at the junior college, until you get it all straight.

JOEL. Open your present. *(She does.)* We'll have a great summer. I'll tell you the truth about how I'm doing. Then *(She unfurls her present, a State University pennant.)* you have to go to State. You can't let this hurt you, too. That would be worse for me.

DEMON *(moving toward JULIE, it reaches, touches the space around her head affectionately. Quietly)*. Joel… Look at her. You called her back to you. You know why. You won't hurt anymore. *(JOEL looks at JULIE. This is what she's been waiting for.)*

JULIE. Jacob?

HOLLY *(sings through to the end, from "Dreams")*.
**I HEAR SOME VOICES CALLING
FROM A DISTANT SHORE.
I KNOW IT SOUNDS FAMILIAR
FROM SOMEWHERE BEFORE.
I'M MAKING FOR THE OCEAN
AND MY DREAMS ARE ON THE TIDE.
THE VOICE WAS MY TOMORROWS
THAT I HAD LOCKED INSIDE.
SINGING, NEVER WILL WE EVER, EVER BE
DENIED.**

(JOEL moves to JULIE. She sees him coming, stands. She suddenly embraces him. LUCAS sees JOEL with JULIE, moves to them, pulls JOEL away from JULIE.)

JULIE. Jacob.

LUCAS *(pulls JOEL center)*. Joel.

JOEL. Yeah?

LUCAS. Thanks for the apartment. I couldn't go without it.

JOEL. I know.

LUCAS. We're going to have a great year.

JOEL. Yeah. *(LUCAS and JOEL stand together until the end.)*

HOLLY *(sings while everyone talks quietly improvising dialogue with the last people they talked with)*.
**'CAUSE I WON'T GIVE UP ON MY DREAMS.
NO, I WON'T GIVE UP ON MY DREAMS
YOU SAY "YOU'RE OUT OF YOUR MIND.
TO LEAVE IT ALL BEHIND."**
(JOEL embraces LUCAS, they freeze.)
BUT I WON'T GIVE UP ON MY DREAMS—
(All freeze. Dim-out, as HOLLY's last chord dies out.)

THE END

AFTERWORD

For this play, it was a clear choice of mine not to include any adults. This presented challenges, considering the subject matter of some of the play.

But I was writing a drama to be performed in the high school, by high school actors. The commissioners asked to keep the adult roles to a minimum. They wished to cast the important roles—all roles if possible—age appropriately, with their students. This would focus the entire play on the young characters—their experiences, their perceptions. Any adult perceptions would have to be filtered through them.

A number of years ago, I worked on a twelve-bed acute-care psychiatric ward. I must confess it feels somewhat unrealistic, in certain moments in this play, for the staff not to appear in the day room, especially when someone is experiencing an emotional crises.

However, by excluding staff, the young people in the play are forced to deal with whatever arises themselves (as they often did on the ward). I felt it would reveal more to us about the young people, in a more efficient way, in a more dramatic way, than if interrupted by the hospital staff.

Also, I wanted the play focused as little as possible on the mental-health system. I wished to focus more on issues in the characters themselves, all the characters, and on this particular period in their lives.

Of course, the characters themselves do have the benefit of the complete hospital staff and other adults. But we don't see the fact of their interactions, only the effects of them.

Also, I've taken out most of the diagnostic references. I found these distracting. In the hospital, on the ward, it seemed that diagnostics was an inexact science—albeit an important element in treatment. But I found, by including diagnostic references in the play, they sometimes seem to limit the perception of audience members. The specific diagnostic labels seemed to contain inflexible connotations. And some audience would focus on the diagnosis at the expense of the full character. In addition, there would be irrelevant, fruitless discussion about the correct diagnosis of a given character.

Coby is not manic depressive (bipolar), nor is she delusional or suicidal. Moreover, she frequently has her attention out on other people and demonstrates a genuine positive regard for them and their success in the world (especially Trisha).

Katherine's movements: as pointed out in the text, although she is catatonic, Katherine can be led. The best way is to walk arm in arm, side by side, pulling her along. She will walk slowly, rigidly, stiffly—but she does not lurch. At no time, while Katherine is catatonic, when Coby moves Katherine's arms or hands, is she limp or does she move quickly. There is always stiffened resistance.

As stated in the text, Joel's drums are basically a single person playing a complete drum set rhythmically, musically. The drums keep a strong rock and roll beat that Joel can follow—with crescendos and flourishes—that is not too fast and never frenetic. The drums must fit the rhythms in the scene and build as the scene builds.

Please do not expand the Voices electronically, such as adding reverb or echo to them. This will tend to dominate too many moments of the show, as well as present an inaccurate statement about Joel's Voices.

When Joel and the Ghost speak and move together, the more interesting the choreography, the more compelling the moment becomes.

— Max Bush
March 2004

Dreams

Dale Dieleman

Driving Rock

It's said if you can dream it, you can make it real

Life as you per - ceive it has its own ap - peal I have no il - lu-sions of a

fu - ture in this place. I won't trade my to - mor-rows for your sweet and smi - ling

face, and I'm feel-ing like a dan-cer who is run-ning out of space _____ Cause I

Chorus Won't give up on my dreams, _____ No, I won't give up on my dreams. _

_ You say you're out of your mind, _ to leave it all be - hind, but I won't give

2003

Dreams

up   on my   dreams _____   Oooo - Oooo - Ooo - - -

Fine last time

Won't give up ____ on my   dreams _____   I   hear some voi - ces

call - ing   from a dis - tant shore.   I   know it sounds fa - mi - liar

from some-where be   fore.   I'm ma-king for the   o - cean and my   dreams are on the

tide,   the   voice was my to - mor-rows that - I had locked in side.   Sing-ing

ne - ver will we   e - ver,   e - ver be de - ni - ed.   Cause I

Over Water

Words and Music by Dale Dieleman

2003

Over Water

DIRECTOR'S NOTES

DIRECTOR'S NOTES